VIRTUOUS LIVES

VIRTUOUS LIVES

Four Quaker Sisters
Remember Family Life,
Abolitionism, and Women's Suffrage

Lucille Salitan
Eve Lewis Perera,
Editors

CONTINUUM • NEW YORK

1994
The Continuum Publishing Company
370 Lexington Avenue, New York, NY 10017

Printed in the United States of America

Library of Congress Cataloging-in-Publication Data

Virtuous lives : four Quaker sisters remember family life,
    abolitionism, and women's suffrage / Lucille Salitan and
    Eve Lewis Perera, editors.
        p. cm.
    Rev. ed. of: Two Quaker sisters, 1937.
    Contents: Reminiscences of childhood / by Elizabeth Buffum Chace
— Some recollections of her girlhood / by Lydia Buffum Read — Diary
Excerpts / by Lucy Buffum Lovell — A visit to John Brown in 1859 /
written by Rebecca Buffum Spring — A slave's escape / by James Curry
as told to Elizabeth Buffum Chace — Letters to family, friends, and the
Providence journal / by Elizabeth Buffum Chace — An address on
women's suffrage / by Elizabeth Buffum Chace —Factory working
conditions for women and girls / by Elizabeth Buffum Chace.
    ISBN 0-8264-0687-4 (pbk. : alk. paper)
    1. Quaker women—New England—Diaries. 2. Quaker women—
New England—Correspondence. 3. Buffum family—Diaries. 4. Buffum
family—Correspondence. 5. Women—Suffrage—United States—
History—19th century. 6. Antislavery movements—United States—
History—19th century. I. Salitan, Lucille. II. Perera, Eve Lewis. III.
Chace, Elizabeth Buffum, 1806–1899. IV. Read, Lydia Buffum. V.
Lovell, Lucy Buffum. VI. Spring, Rebecca Buffum. VII. Two Quaker
sisters.

F15. F89V57 1994   94-21307
947'.0088286—dc20   CIP

Contents

Acknowledgments

The editors wish to thank the following people for their assistance in the preparation of this book: Mark Brown and the staff at the John Hay Library of Brown University, the staff at the Rhode Island Historical Society, Malcolm Lovell, Arnold Lovell, Malcolm Chace, Dr. Richard Perera, Angela Lampiasi, Terry Post, and our editor at Continuum, Cynthia Eller.

Introduction

*U*nder the title *Two Quaker Sisters,* the original edition of this book was published in 1937, becoming a *New York Times* best-seller. In the foreword to that edition the Buffum era was characterized as an age that seemed strangely primitive. However, some fifty-seven years later we see in these stories an extraordinary similarity and relevance to many of the most pressing and persistent social and moral problems of our time written in a style that conveys a vividness and intimacy rarely found in contemporary literature.

Both of us have a keen interest in early American domestic history, and have been involved in activities for social change and justice. When we discovered that we both owned and prized copies of this rare book we felt compelled to seek publication of a second edition since two generations have grown up without the opportunity to savor this poignant first-hand account of nineteenth-century life in rural New England. Although different in so many ways from today, the Buffum era is also familiar in its humanity which casts a seductive spell on our imaginations. There are important lessons that can be learned from these four sisters who cherished the ideal of living virtuous lives: lessons about the value of strength of character, moral seriousness, family solidarity, commitment to ideals, and the rewards of hard work, good citizenship, and a simple lifestyle.

The early and middle years of the nineteenth century were full of excess and violence, of social and political upheaval and religious fervor. It was during this period that the Buffum sisters were young women raising large families and participating in the liberal social and political movements of the day. It was a time when women were generally denied economic and political rights and were excluded from debates about public issues. But these were Quaker women, whose tradition did not exclude them. It encouraged and educated them to play an active, and often a leadership role in public affairs, as they had from the beginning in the affairs of their religious society and its institutions.

When George Fox founded the Society of Friends in mid-seventeenth-century England, he preached that the Divine Light was within everyone. Therefore, no intermediary was necessary for an individual to experience the Holy Spirit and learn the ways of righteous conduct. When Fox married Margaret Fell, a natural leader, they encouraged women's meetings, thus placing women on an equal footing with men in the Society. It was not long after that that women became preachers and spokespersons for these, at the time, quite heretical beliefs.

The Quakers stubbornly resisted many common customs as being reflective of rigid class distinctions in society. They refused to pay tithes or to swear an oath. They would not remove their hats as a sign of deference. They insisted on wearing plain clothes, and used the plain speech of working people, preferring the familiar and more democratic "thee" to the formal "you." They addressed everyone by their given name or the combination of given and surname, eschewing the use of titles. They rejected the common names of the days and months as pagan in origin. Instead, they used numerical designations (as in "First Day" for Sunday).

The Friends saw their movement as a third manifestation of Christianity, alongside Catholicism and Protestantism, defining themselves as seekers of the truth. Their religious revolution began during the era of Cromwell's Protectorate, and the anti-royalist sentiments of the day probably strengthened their commitment to fervently pursue social justice. They combined Christian trinitarian beliefs with practical worldly efforts by living them through their participation in liberal social causes.

Their mystical beliefs were not only individual, but were experienced in union with others during their silent worship service or Meeting. Still, they respected the right of each individual to maintain his or her personal convictions. They emphasized the value of education and teaching more than belief in miracles; if one follows the light within, they said, one can learn to distinguish truth from falsehood and right from wrong. This does not mean, however, that all Quakers agree on all matters. On the contrary, there was then and is today great divergence of thought among people who claim to be Quakers, running the gamut from extreme conservatism to radical liberalism.

In the early years of the movement, Quakers suffered violent persecution from the Church of England and from the Puritans. They were imprisoned and fined: Fox estimated that in the years from 1654 to 1656 there were seldom less than 1000 Quakers in prison. They began to leave England for North America in the last half of the seventeenth century. Unfortunately, in New England, where strict laws were passed against them, they found even more persecution. The first arrivals were two women, Ann Austin and Mary Fisher, who were imprisoned and then deported. Others were flogged and driven from town to town, and four, including one woman, are known to have been hanged. After being expelled from Massachusetts and Connecticut, they found refuge in Rhode Island were Roger Williams had established a colony on the principle of absolute religious freedom.

In the nineteenth century the Quakers passed through a time of quietism when many members withdrew from worldly activities and many Meetings established strict supervision over their members' private lives. Disownments—as expulsions from the Society were called—were enforced for such infringements as marriage to a non-Quaker or speaking out too stridently against injustice. This narrowness of viewpoint and harshness of discipline resulted in the loss of many prominent members and reduced the Friends' numbers and their prestige. There were also internal schisms between the Orthodox and the Hicksites and the Gurneyites and Wilberites from

1827 to 1840 which further weakened the Society. Ironically, this provided Quaker women with an opportunity to participate more fully in the political and social movements that dominated secular affairs, and the Buffum sisters were among those women.

Although Quaker men and women worshipped together on First Day, they held separate monthly and quarterly meetings that attended to business matters, and it was the experience of organizing and managing these meetings that provided the circumstances for women to develop their strengths and leadership abilities. These carried over eventually into their secular activities, and led to their considerable impact on the societal changes that occurred with the abolition of slavery, and the struggle for women's right to vote. Quaker women, although only a fraction of the total population, often made up one-fourth or more of the numbers in the anti-slavery and suffrage movements. From the beginning they stood firmly in opposition to war, and protested against all forms of violence and injustice through their activities in education and relief work. These activities continue to the present day.

The diaries and reminiscences written by the Buffum sisters, although unusual for that period, are very much in the tradition of the nineteenth-century Quaker life, reflecting the attitudes and activities of the Society and the intimate details of family life. The Buffum stories depict the simple domestic life of a leading Rhode Island family who lived most of their lives in New England, who married New Englanders and whose characters, convictions, and actions were founded on a long line of pioneering New England Quakers and especially upon strong independent-minded women.

The sisters' first ancestor in America was Robert Buffum who, with his wife Tamasine, came to these shores from Yorkshire, England in 1632 and settled in Salem, Massachusetts. Robert joined the Quakers late in life at a time when they were the most unpopular and most persecuted sect in America. His earnestness and independence of character have been reflected in his descendants through the generations. At Robert's death the Salem authorities refused to probate his will due to the refusal of his children—all good Quakers—to swear an oath to the witnessing of the documents. Therefore, one heir was forced to go to England where he had to appeal to the authorities to right this "monstrous injustice."

Many of Robert's children and grandchildren were persecuted by the Salem magistrates and were mentioned many times as "troublesome and pestilent Quakers." One daughter was tied to a cart and publicly whipped for criticizing some acts of the municipal government. The eldest son was imprisoned for spreading Quaker propaganda and was banished from the state on pain of death.

Robert's great-grandson was Joseph, who married Margaret Osborne and moved from Salem to Smithfield, Rhode Island around 1740, by then a haven for Quakers. There he made a clearing, built a house and prospered as a farmer, a miller, and a manufacturer of cloth while raising fourteen children.

Joseph's third son William married Lydia Arnold, inherited the property in Smithfield, and developed the manufacturing business. He became interested in the slavery question and joined the Rhode Island Society for the Gradual Abolition of Slavery: a strategy that his granddaughters would later oppose in favor of immediate abolition.

William's eldest son Thomas was also a successful farmer and manufacturer. In later life he became one of Rhode Island's outstanding jurists, serving as Associate Judge of the Supreme Court until he resigned because of his unwillingness to pronounce the death sentence in cases of manslaughter: the only punishment that the law then allowed.

William's second son Arnold, father of the sisters whose writings form this volume, married Sarah Gould in 1803. They had ten children, of whom seven lived to maturity. Arnold was a farmer and manufacturer, and also an inventor and lecturer. As a farmer he upheld the traditions of his ancestors, but was not inclined toward working the land, being more interested in the manufacturing of hats (for which he invented many devices to improve existing machinery). However, his main work in life was as an Abolitionist leader.

Bred as he had been in an atmosphere of moral repugnance to slavery, Arnold Buffum early showed intense interest in bringing an end to this injustice, and lectured and worked throughout his life to arouse public sentiment against it. Through this work he met William Lloyd Garrison, and in 1832, along with eleven other distinguished men, founded the New England Anti-Slavery Society, becoming its first president. For the rest of his life Arnold was devoted to this cause, traveling continuously on its behalf until his death. His labors took him throughout New England and the eastern seaboard and west to Ohio and Indiana. He also made several trips abroad to enlist the sympathies and support of the English and the French.

He and his family suffered social ostracism due to the intense feelings in and outside the Quaker community against Abolitionist agitation. The Quakers had emancipated their own slaves but had many close commercial connections with the South and feared detrimental consequences to their businesses. Arnold refused to yield or slacken his efforts when he was warned by the Friends to give up his lecturing, and accordingly was disowned by his Meeting. Deeply hurt, but devoutly religious, he continued to attend meetings and raise his children in the faith.

Arnold had seven children. His eldest son, William, married Marian Simmons. She was the daughter of the Boston merchant John Simmons, who left his fortune to found and endow Simmons College. His second son, Edward, married Eliza Wilkinson, became a reporter for the *New York Herald*, fought in the Mexican War, joined the Gold Rush in California, became a newspaper editor before being elected to the California Legislature, and spent his later years as a foreign correspondent in France.

Arnold's five daughters were Sarah, Elizabeth, Lucy, Rebecca, and Lydia. Sarah married Nathaniel Borden, a manufacturer, and Mayor of Fall River, Massachusetts. Elizabeth married Samuel Chace, also from Fall River, and they moved to Valley Falls, Rhode Island in 1839. There her husband and his brother founded a cotton manufacturing business that made them wealthy and influential industrialists. The success of the Chace enterprise freed Elizabeth from much domestic responsibility to use her considerable talent of leadership in the liberal social causes in which she was involved. Their home became a meeting place for the prominent liberal thinkers of the day. For many years it was also used as a station on the Underground Railroad, assisting slaves to travel to Canada and freedom.

All of the sisters and their families helped in this work, which put them in great danger after the Fugitive Slave Act of 1850 was passed by Congress. If caught, violators were subject to heavy fines and imprisonment, not to mention enormous social stigma. Often it was necessary to hide slaves in the cellar for a week or more before the furor of the hunt had died down enough to permit them to proceed safely on the journey north.

In later years, after the emancipation, Elizabeth devoted her time and talents to such liberal causes as women's suffrage, prison reform, temperance, and improvement of the working conditions of women and girls in the New England mills. A founding member of the Rhode Island Woman's Suffrage Association, she served as its president for twenty-seven years, and in 1882 was elected president of the national association.

Of Elizabeth's ten children, the first five died in infancy; she then bore five more, but only three lived to maturity. Her son Arnold continued the cotton business and became chancellor of Brown University for twenty-five years. Her daughter Mary married Horace Cheney and later James Tolman. Daughter Lillie, who wrote a two-volume biography of her mother, married Arthur Crawford Wyman.

Lucy married a Baptist minister, the Rev. Nehemiah Lovell. Like the Buffums and the Chaces, he had deep roots in New England, his ancestors having arrived on the Mayflower. Arnold Buffum did not forbid the marriage, although many Quaker fathers would have done so. Unlike her sisters, Lucy had few material luxuries, having to manage on her husband's salary of $400 a year. She had six children, of whom the first three died in infancy. The surviving three were William, Shubael, and Lucy. When her husband of sixteen years died, leaving her alone to raise small children, she opened a grammar school where she taught for many years.

Rebecca married Marcus Spring, a wealthy New York merchant, and Lydia married Clement Read. These two sisters were especially fond of each other, and when the Springs founded an intentional community in Eagleswood, New Jersey, Lydia, with her husband and daughter, Sarah, moved there. Called the "Raritan Bay Union" this idealistic community was made up of anti-slavery liberals along with artists and literary people. Sarah Read, Lydia' s daughter, eventually married Lucy's son William Lovell, her first cousin. Their son Malcom compiled the first edition of these papers.

When we decided to pursue an expanded edition, we contacted direct descendants of Elizabeth and Lucy, Malcolm Chace, and Malcolm and Arnold Lovell, who were most helpful in assisting us in

locating the original documents. We consequently spent many pleasant hours reading through the voluminous diaries, letters, essays,
speeches, journals, and news clippings family members had left to
the archives at the John Hay Library of Brown University. The
amount of material is extraordinary, and it is hard to comprehend
how such busy, active women found time to record so much about
their lives. Fortunately for us they did. What is published here is but
a small portion of that material. To the original text we have added
recollections of early childhood by the youngest sister, Lydia; and
accounts by Elizabeth regarding the women's suffrage movement,
the plight of women factory workers, and letters she wrote to family, friends, and the *Providence Journal.* (Apparently, like us, she was
a prolific writer of letters to the editor.)

      We hope you will find as much value and inspiration in these
stories as we do, and as much pleasure in getting to know the Buffum
sisters as we do in presenting them to you.

                                                    LUCILLE SALITAN
                                                    EVE LEWIS PERERA

• 1 •

Reminiscences of Childhood

by Elizabeth Buffum Chace,
Written in 1897

*W*hen the time comes that men and women shall better understand the laws of heredity, there will come also a stronger sense of
responsibility concerning the characteristics with which they shall
endow their offspring.

Having during my life of ninety-one years been personally
acquainted with five generations of the descendants of Joseph and
Margaret Buffum, I have been led to notice in every family certain
inherited qualities of character.

My great-grandmother Margaret Osborne Buffum was the daughter
of William Osborne of Danvers. She married my great-grandfather
Joseph Buffum, near the middle of the eighteenth century, and went
to live with him in Smithfield, Rhode Island.

Before her first child was born she went to her own home in
Danvers to put herself under the care of her mother, making the

journey of fifty miles on horseback through what must have been at that time nearly a wilderness, where she remained until after the birth of the child, and then returned to Smithfield with the child in her arms, again on horseback. Before the birth of the second child, there still being no neighbors in the settlement of Smithfield upon whom she could depend for aid, she made the same journey in the same way, carrying the first child with her, and after the birth returning with both children. It is to be supposed that her husband made all the journeys with her, but of that tradition saith not.

She was a person of more than ordinary ability, physically of a large frame and of commanding presence. She had fourteen children, eight sons and six daughters, whom she brought up to be steady industrious men and women and all of whom lived to be married and with families of their own, and to each of whom their father gave a farm.

Then, after raising all of her own children, she took eight destitute children and brought them up in her own house.

She was a woman of more than ordinary mental strength and positiveness. She had a high sense of justice and great administrative ability, but there was a severity in her treatment of her children which may have aroused a spirit of rebellion, and which probably extended to a number of apprentices for whom she cared, and made their lives not so comfortable as they might have been under a gentler authority. Still, all persons who knew her regarded her with much respect for her judgment and the soundness of her advice.

One day, when she was whipping with a horsewhip a half-grown son in the yard, a neighbor came along, and stepping through the open gate, called out to the boy, "Run, Dick, run!" She turned towards the intruder and exclaimed, "Stand out of the way or I'll put it on to thee."

Tradition says that this woman whipped every one of her sons after he was twenty-one years old.

My great-grandfather Joseph was a member of the Society of Friends and attended Friends Meeting. His wife Margaret was a Presbyterian and went to church in the neighboring town of Uxbridge. After there were children old enough to go, and they used to go very young in those days, my great-grandfather bought a chaise, the first seen in the town.

On First Day morning he would harness the horse and help his wife and the children into the chaise, start them off to church, and then walk himself two miles to the Friends Meeting.

One morning on her way to church my grandmother was impressed with the conviction that it was her duty thereafter to go to church with her husband, and so she did, and became a member of the Society, and their children were brought up therein.

Joseph Buffum owned all the land now occupied by the Village of Slatersville. He had a saw mill and grist mill in addition to the large farming business which he carried on. The manner of life at this farm was primitive and patriarchal. The employees in the mill, forge, and store all formed a part of the household.

The town was then very sparsely populated, so that in her new home my great-grandmother had few neighbors, and those not very near.

In this house, besides the ordinary housework of those days, various manufactures were carried on: candle making, soap making, butter and cheese making, spinning, weaving, dyeing, and of course all the knitting and sewing, the dressmaking and tailoring, and probably the shoe making and the millinery of this large household were performed within its limits—and the children, whether native or adopted, began very early to do their share.

To his wife's administrative ability Joseph Buffum attributed much of his success in life. A granddaughter of hers who remembered her well, told me that she was the nurse, the lawyer, the doctor and the counselor of all the people dwelling for miles around and that no man among them would have bought or sold a farm or entered into any new business without consulting "Aunt Margaret," as she was universally called.

The many workmen on the farm were called to their meals by her strong clear voice, no horn or bell being necessary.

The village where they lived, now called Union Village, bears the marks of age, but the old fashioned structure of its buildings, its ample dooryards, its venerable trees retain a general air of stateliness and simple elegance which, although now somewhat faded, show that it has been the abode of a rural aristocracy that inherited the tastes and customs of Colonial neatness and prosperity.

At the time of which I write, between the years of 1810 and 1825, it bore the Indian name Woonsocket, from the hill at the foot of which it lay, while the place now claiming that title was simply The Falls, the Blackstone River making there a precipitous descent.

During these years the village included in its social relations all the inhabitants of nearly three miles of land, who probably numbered not over a thousand souls. Some of them were descendants of Quakers exiled from Massachusetts in the time of the Puritanic Persecutions, and most of them were connected by membership or sympathy with the Society of Friends.

A house of worship of this Society was the only public building, except a steepled schoolhouse that was called the Academy.

The road from Providence to Worcester ran through the place, and two rival taverns furnished rest and refreshment to travelers passing through in the stagecoaches or private carriages. Public gatherings for political purposes or for purposes of entertainment or amusement were held in the halls of the taverns, in one of which was the town library. The post office was kept in a private house. The Smithfield Union Bank was a small red building in the centre of the village. The business was mainly farming; the farms running back from the street to the hills on one side, and to the river on the other.

The finest residences, those of the wealthiest citizens scattered over these three miles, were large farm houses, usually painted either white or yellow, but here and there a red house varied the monotony; and in most cases there were green blinds on the windows. When the blinds were lacking, curtains made of woven rushes were used. The woodwork and the walls inside were painted, and there was a good deal of wainscoting. Houses of poorer families were constructed much after the same pattern, but were smaller and more cheaply finished. They were all rectangular in form and low studded. There were no Queen Anne imitations.

The front door of my grandfather's house was entered through a portico, which had seats on each side and was floored by broad, flat stones, such as also made a walk extending through the dooryard. This yard was surrounded by a picket fence.

The house itself had a hall running from front to back, with an outside door at either end. Two front rooms were large and square, a parlor and a sitting room which was also the dining room. The two back rooms, from which closets were taken, were bedrooms, one for the father and mother and the other for the best guest chamber. The second story was divided into bedrooms for the children and for guests, large provision being made for both. The top floor was a great open garret, surmounted by two chimneys, the only means of heating being by open wood fireplaces in the rooms below. I do not remember any inside shutters. I think every front door had a knocker; evolution had not brought the bell. There were no bay windows nor piazzas.

The kitchen was in a lower structure, also of two stories, built on as an addition, square, and crowned with another chimney which carried the smoke from a huge fireplace in which, with its brick ovens, were cooked the most elaborate dinners and breakfasts imaginable.

In the best houses the furniture was largely mahogany, large heavy chairs with and without arms, with flag seats and no upholstery but with loose homemade cushions, some with rockers but none with castors, and all with very straight stiff backs. The sofa had not been developed there in Smithfield, and the center table had not arrived. The small round stand was common and occasionally there stood in a corner or at one side of the room, a small table the top of which turned up on a hinge. In one corner of the sitting room stood the tall eight-day clock, and beside it, in the best houses, hung a barometer and a thermometer in one frame.

The fireplace was embellished by large brass andirons and their adjuncts, and it was with pride that the skillful housemothers selected for their sitting rooms the smooth back logs and the straight proper-sized foresticks, and so tended their fires and used their hearth brushes, that the evening fireside was always handsome and inviting. Brass candlesticks held the only lighting apparatus of those earlier years.

The bedsteads were high from the floor and in the best rooms had tall posts from which curtains were suspended. Feather beds were in common use, and patchwork quilts and homemade blankets were the coverings. Beautiful handwoven linen was common for sheets and pillow cases. Carpets were unknown in those early years of my childhood. I think about the year 1812 the wealthiest man in the region married for his third wife a highbred Nantucket lady, who in a short time had a handsome carpet laid on her parlor floor. It was the only one that I remember to have seen in any house before 1824. Ordinarily parlor and sitting-room floors were painted in the mode called "marbled."

My grandfather William Buffum, the third son of Joseph and Margaret Buffum, was the only one of the many sons and daughters of Joseph and Margaret Buffum who remained in the village where he was born. He married Lydia Arnold and settled on a farm adjoining his paternal home and built and occupied a house where they reared their four sons and five daughters.

This house has been preserved so well that it now bears the same respectable and aristocratic appearance, with its long low frame, its low ceilings, its wainscoting, its great open garret, as when I, as a child, spent half my growing years with the dear grandparents whose home it was and from whose hospitable doors had gone forth the sons and daughters who constituted a distinguished portion of the inhabitants up and down those country roads between Slatersville and The Falls.

My grandfather was a member of the Rhode Island Society for the Gradual Abolition of Slavery, thus taking an initial step in the great struggle to which his son Arnold, my father, devoted so much of his time and energy. When my grandfather's children were young his house was a refuge for fugitive slaves from New York, slavery having been abolished in Rhode Island in 1784. At one time a whole family of fugitive slaves came to his farm and he settled them there and took them into his employ. Rhode Island law at that time permitted owners to claim any escaped slaves, and the owner of this Negro family one day came and solicited help from local officers of the law. Accompanied by several of the officers, the slave owner went to the farm. There he met my grandfather surrounded by a group of his white employees, all fully armed and determined to protect the black refugees. So fierce was the attitude of the Quakers and so evident their willingness to use the weapons prohibited to their faith, that the officers, their heart not in their mission anyway, retreated, and the slave owner, of necessity, as well. The slaves remained on the farm for many years as free hired employees.

Years later in Boston in 1832 my father Arnold Buffum founded and became the first president of the New England Anti-Slavery Society, and William Lloyd Garrison was its secretary.

Lydia, my grandmother, was a woman of very different type from her mother-in-law. While she was perhaps nearly as skillful in managing her household, her most striking characteristics were gentle, womanly qualities, which endeared her strongly to her children and neighbors. She was known in her more mature years throughout the neighborhood as "Aunt Lydia." Her voice was soft and mild and her manner sweet and graceful. With all her mildness she was, according to the custom of the time, undemonstrative of affection. I was, I believe, her favorite grandchild, but I have no recollection of her ever giving me a kiss in all my growing years. On the other hand, though I spent a good part of my time with her from my eighth to my seventeenth year, I do not remember ever hearing an impatient word escape her lips.

My grandfather always addressed his wife as "my dear," and never by her name, and I have heard him often say in his old age, "My wife and I have lived together sixty years, and in all that time she has never spoken a word to me but in the pleasantest manner possible."

A little while before her death, when in a partially paralyzed condition, this dear woman dictated an address to be written to her numerous children, particularly those who were married, urging them to live in undying love towards one another and not to allow themselves to get into the habit of speaking in an unpleasant way. I do not know what became of this document.

Looking down the years to the four succeeding generations following hers, I can see in the descendants some marked cases of sweetness of disposition transmitted from her.

When I knew my grandmother she always wore a mob cap made of plain and sheer white muslin and tied under her chin. She never wore a gown made of any material that could not be washed, but always what was called a "stuff" gown. The skirt was open from the waist, being made without any front breadth, and it was worn over a dark petticoat of very much the same color and texture as itself. Over this, so as to conceal the opening in the skirt, she wore a long apron, and she folded a square white muslin kerchief around her neck.

She had much love of ornamenting her house. Her daughters used to raise silkworms. She saved the yellow egg-shaped cocoons and made them up to look like canary birds, and put them among the branches of asparagus with which she decorated her ceilings. She cultivated the garden flowers common in those days, roses, sweet williams, and pinks, and in every way she filled the home with sweetness.

To us, the numerous grandchildren, no pleasure exceeded our visits to the dear grandparents. Of course I did not know my grandmother until most of her children had left the parental roof.

William Buffum, my grandfather, had a disposition softer and more mellow than that of his mother Margaret's, but still he was always an impatient man, and although I have no remembrance of ever seeing him actually cross or angry, he was always nervous and worried when things did not go to suit him.

He brought up and trained a boy taken from a poor but respectable family and set him on his feet as a working man and then took another lad from the same family. One Second Day morning when I was a child I passed through the kitchen where this boy was pounding clothes. He had been out until late the night before and he was then refusing to tell my grandfather where he had been. "Where wast thou?" my grandfather demanded. The boy replied that he went out with one of the men. "Where didst thou go?" asked the questioner, and still the boy would not say. In a tone that could not be disregarded the old man said, "Thou must and shall tell or quit here." Then the boy confessed that he and his companion went to a disreputable house in the village near by. What followed I did not learn, but for some reason this little scene impressed me strongly. I never knew the measure of discipline my grandfather had been accustomed to use with his own children, but in this case he apparently felt the responsibility to be wise in his guardianship, and I think he did not strike the boy.

William Buffum's ordinary manner was truly majestic and worthy of his mother. I seem to see him now in his suit of drab broadcloth, consisting of a coat and vest, and smallclothes buckled at the knee; he wore a drab broad-brimmed hat and long knit stockings gartered above the knee. In the house he wore low shoes with buckles, and out of doors fair-topped boots. It was the Quakers' usual attire, and my father, though a young man, wore the same costume at that time. Fair-topped boots were those made of dark leather to the knee, where they were finished off by a sort of cuff of light-colored leather, which was turned down over the leg of the boot, making a band supposed to be ornamental around its top.

My grandfather was a director in the Smithfield Union Bank, two miles away from his home, and never did I know him, even when an old man, to fail in attendance upon the directors' meeting at two o'clock every Sixth Day. At one-half past one o'clock his chaise, which was the first one owned in the community, was brought to the front gate. He took his whip from its place behind the tall clock in the sitting room and departed with unvarying punctuality.

One day when he was ready to start, his whip could not be found, and he immediately became agitated and impatient. Grandmother trotted around in her feeble way, for she was then an old woman, but calm and serene as she always was, while he went from corner to corner fretting and declaring that somebody had displaced the whip, and he should never see it again. Meanwhile, I, a child nine years old, was directed to run here and there and was made to feel almost that I was the culprit who had caused all the trouble. Finally the lost article was found and he hurried away, averring that he should be late for the meeting. As the door closed behind him, I exclaimed impulsively, "I'm glad he's gone!" The moment I had spoken I was frightened, and I looked up at grandmother, expecting a rebuke. With her usual sweet serenity but in a somewhat pathetic tone, "So am I," she said, to my great relief.

During my childhood the girl who did the housework was a daughter of a sister of my grandfather who lived in New Hampshire. Two more of the same family lived as "hired girls" in the families of two of my uncles. They were not called servants, and were members of the family, eating at table with them, but they did an enormous amount of work and did it well. At my grandfather's the girl's day began at four o'clock in the morning with the heating of the oven in which in addition to a variety of other "victuals" the most delicious Indian cakes were baked for breakfast.

Cheese-making, the churning of butter, and candle-making were a part of the duties of the hired girl while the spinning-wheel stood in the kitchen to be put in motion in any spare moments. As this particular girl was unusually good she was paid a dollar and a half a week.

A building in the backyard had a basement, where cotton yarn was dyed before being woven into ginghams and the upper story was a tenement for a workman's family. Here a room was reserved to hold a loom, and an extra woman was often employed as a weaver.

My grandmother Lydia herself, when quite an old woman used to spin flax on a low linen wheel. Patience, my father's eldest sister, when a young girl, raised silkworms, wound the silk from the cocoons, doubled and twisted it, had it dyed, wove it herself, and made it into a gown in which she was married in 1793 to Pliny Earle. I have a piece of the silk still, but it was woven long before my day.

One of my earliest memories is connected with the silkworms which my aunts raised, and the first recollection I have of my grandparents belongs to a day when I was perhaps three years old and I was visiting their house with other relatives. A cousin of my father's carried me on his shoulder to the carriage house to look at the silkworms. He stood there holding me and talking to me about the worms, and I looked at some geese that were running about the floor, and I thought they were the worms. Indeed, it was many years before, as a consequence of this infantile mistake, I ever got the ideas of silkworms and of geese quite disassociated in my mind.

In my childhood we wore in summer imported calico and muslin frocks and in winter dresses of a homemade material composed of cotton warp with woolen weft or filling—usually the warp was blue and the filling red, though the prettiest was when the warp was white.

Our frocks—my sisters' and mine—when I was from eight to twelve years old, were made low in the neck and were tied with strings in the back, as were our petticoats. Sometimes they were pinned. There were no buttons, and hooks and eyes came later. I think we had no boughten tape at that time; for strings we braided "thrums" which were the ends of the warp left by the weavers. This braiding was the children's work.

In those days all the stockings were knit by the women. Knitting was their evening work, and as only candles were used for lighting it was fortunate that it could be done almost in darkness. The hired girls spun and twisted the yarn in the kitchens.

My mother had such a houseful of little girls, five at that time, that my grandmother Buffum used to keep me with her about half the time; and when there, what I needed of clothing she provided. I think it was in the year 1815 that a worsted material called bombazet was first imported into this country and a cousin of mine, whose father was a wealthy man had a bombazet frock for her best instead of the usual linsey-woolsey. I was then nine years old, and I longed for a bombazet frock. I don't think I begged for it, for children in those days were not allowed as much freedom of choice as they are now, but I suppose I let my desire be known; however, my grandmother was economical, and she compromised by getting me a heavy Scotch gingham, with a pretty large check of blue and white. I seem to see it now, for I didn't like it, though it was supposed to be nicer than the customary linsey-woolsey. The first time I wore this frock to Meeting, it had been arranged that I should go home with my cousin who had the bombazet and spend the afternoon, and be sent for at night. So with my Quaker bonnet and my outside garment called a coat, which reached below my frock, I went in a dissatisfied state of mind to meeting. I was a religious child, and a reader of the Bible. I had been well instructed in the duty of worship and of serious reflection in Meeting. But my poor little heart was sore, and I tried to turn my worship to account. I had read "Ask and ye shall receive; seek and ye shall find"; "If ye have faith ye shall remove mountains"; "The fervent effectual prayer of the righteous man availeth much." And in the faith so implanted, I spent the hour of the silent meeting in fervent prayer that my gingham dress might be changed to bombazet. I am not sure that I felt entire confidence, but I had strong hope and a good degree of faith. My coat entirely covered the frock, so I could not see the process of change. I went home with my cousin. I took off my coat in excitement and agitation, and there was my gingham dress just the same. I said nothing, children kept their heartaches more to themselves then than they do now, and it was many years before I ever told the story, or ever suffered a deeper disappointment.

White flour was used at my grandfather's only to make pie crust, cake, and such delicacies. It was bought only in quantities of seven pounds at a time. Rye flour and Indian meal were used to make the bread which was ordinarily eaten. When the oldest boy, Thomas, was six or seven years of age, they used to put a sack of corn across the back of a horse, seat the child firmly in the middle, and send him to the miller, where the horse would stop of its own accord, and the little fellow would cry out: "Somebody come an' take us off!" The miller would take off the child and corn, grind the corn, place the meal in the sack, put it back on the horse, seat Thomas again in the middle, and send him home.

The loaves of rye and the Indian bread were baked on oak leaves. The women spread these leaves on a large wooden shovel, took the dough with their hands from the big wooden trough in which with their hands they had mixed it, molded it into mounds on the leaves, put the shovel into the oven, and dexterously slipped it out again, after depositing dough and leaves upon the oven floor. Indian meal puddings and pies were also baked in the brick oven. It took all night to bake an Indian meal pudding properly. In the autumn the children gathered the oak leaves for baking purposes and strung them on sticks. They called it "leafing."

When the first grist of meal from newly harvested Indian corn was brought home, in the fall, the custom was to make a great quantity of hasty pudding for supper. And on this occasion the hired men, that is, the farm hands who usually ate in the kitchen, were invited into the dining room dressed in their best clothes, to eat the hasty pudding supper with the family. The hired girl was at liberty, if it was convenient, to eat in the dining room at other times.

William Buffum had water brought into his house through log pipes and was the first person in the region to have such a convenience as running water in the kitchen.

When I was two years old I began to be taken to the Quaker Meeting as well as to school. I wore a little silk Quaker bonnet. When I was three years old I could read very well.

I remember well standing, when I was just three and a half, between the knees of a young man who was a cousin of my father's and reading to a large company of Friends from the *Book of Discipline* of our Society, much to their amusement, no doubt, if not to their edification. Their praises of my reading rang in my ears for a long time, and I dare say made me a vain, self-conceited little thing.

At the first school in addition to being taught to read we were taught to sew. At Meeting we were taught to sit still, which in moderation is no mean accomplishment.

After passing through the school for little ones we children— the children in my set in the old village—began receiving our instruction at the Academy. The public school system had not been established in Rhode Island. But our parents were a reading and thinking people, and they intended their children should be well educated.

Several of these parents were the grandchildren of Joseph and Margaret Buffum, and they had themselves been well instructed for their day and generation. They spoke the English language correctly, and I can think of no other reason for the class distinction which did certainly exist in this community, except that it was determined by the different manner in which the language was spoken.

There were families scattered right along this country road owning farms, behaving as irreproachably as their neighbors and dealing as honestly and yet who had no social relations with these same neighbors. They probably used two negatives where there was need of only one, and put plural personal pronouns with singular verbs. They may have belonged to the other political party— our people being all Federalists, the women as well as the men.

There were, during the presidencies of Thomas Jefferson and James Madison, public questions not settled by the Revolutionary War and the organization of the new government. When the weekly news came in the *Manufacturers' and Farmers' Journal* my grandmother was as much interested in everything political as were her husband and the neighboring men. At nine years of age I used to read to my grandparents the whole congressional proceedings and other political matter.

When I was a very little girl I used to be very fond of going off by myself and thinking about things I was not accustomed to hear talked of. One thing in particular was a frequent subject of my mental questioning. "How came there ever to be anything?" and, pursuing, this inquiry, I would penetrate into the great sea of darkness and mystery and try to imagine how it would be if there had never been anything; until I would seem to myself to be so near lost in immensity that I was glad to escape from my solitude and run back to play with the other children, which I was as fond of doing as any of them, and no one ever heard of my searchings into the infinite.

My mother's family, the John Goulds, lived at Newport on the "Island," as we called the Island of Rhode Island. I often visited there and I remember a meeting, when I was eight years old, with one of my father's close friends, William Ellery Channing, who later became known the world over as one of this country's great divines. I was walking alone along a country road when I passed a peach tree laden with particularly luscious fruit. A branch hung over the

stone wall and a beautiful peach waited within reach of my little
arms to be plucked. I was sorely tempted and I picked the fruit and
went along eating it. Just then William Ellery Channing drove by in
a chaise. He pulled up, and in his kindly manner, offered to take me
on my way home. My conscience was very troubled and I poured
out to him the entire story and confessed that I feared I had committed the sin of theft. I remember that he comforted me, but,
stern moralist that he was, he persuaded me to return to the farmhouse where lived the owner of the tree, and confess my guilt to
him and ask his consideration. Fortunately the farmer was a kindly
man who sympathized with me and sent me on with only the softest
of admonitions.

In 1816, when I was ten years old, my father's business caused
a removal to Pomfret, in the State of Connecticut, the land of blue
laws and of Presbyterianism. My sister Lucy and I were sent to the
public school. The scholars were required to salute the teacher as
they entered, and every time they stood before her in the class, with
a bow from the boys and a curtsy from the girls, and in going to and
from school to greet thus every person whom they met on the road.
Our father had instructed us that all such obeisance to human beings
was contrary to the spirit and teachings of Christ, who had forbidden his disciples to call any man Master, and we were cautioned not
to comply with any such custom. Lucy, who was younger than I,
was first called on to make what teacher called her "manners," and
so she was the first to refuse. The teacher threatened to whip her,
and the poor child, too young to understand the principle involved,
could only say, "My father doesn't want me to," and the teacher let
her pass for that day. The next day, my father went and explained,
and so got us excused; but it did not save us from much jeering and
insult from our schoolmates, and, I presume, some disrepute among
our teachers. But we bore it all pretty calmly, for conscience sake.
We were, even at that early age, familiar with persecutions of the
Quakers, both in Old and New England, and we felt in our little
hearts that we were right. We said "thee" though the boys rudely
mocked us, and we were happy in our plain clothes. I can recall no
feeling of regret that we were obliged to appear so different from
the other children, and when they threw our little plain bonnets on
the floor and stamped them out of shape, uttering the opprobrious

name "Quaker" in our ears, I cannot recollect any sorrow beyond that for the spoiling of the bonnets. After a few years we left Connecticut and returned to our old home in Smithfield.

The fathers and mothers in Smithfield had a lively interest in the education of their children, and a good school was maintained fifty-two weeks in the year, with no vacations.

In those days we had school before breakfast and after supper, besides the forenoon and afternoon sessions, and if we did not become profound scholars, it was not for lack of sufficient time devoted to study. For gymnastics, the girls had the sweeping, the chamber work, the bringing of wood from the cellar and making the fires, with the occasional variation of making the boys' beds on busy days; and this last, in our narrow circle of amusements, was considered a privilege. We had no vacations, no holidays; there were no pictures on the walls, no sculptures, no celebrations; we were allowed no curling of the hair, no laces, ruffles, or bright colors upon our garments, no jewelry; our bonnets were largely of wire and pasteboard; and, as for music and singing, why, it almost takes my breath away to hear it now within those walls! And yet it was a good school, where the teachers performed their duties conscientiously; the learning was thorough and solid; and the limitations and restraints, that now are outgrown, were only in excess of what, as "Friends' children," we were accustomed to at home. I do not think as a rule they were considered oppressive, and they certainly were not entirely without some good results. At any rate, I remember well that I left the dear "Stution," as we used to call it, with much sorrow that my school days were over; and good reason have I had since, and still have, to regret that they could not have been prolonged; and at this day I visit the place with a heart full of reverence and love.

Our text books were of a very primitive kind. In geography we had no atlases to use—and I believe the imperfect manner in which I learned localities is the reason why I have never been able to think of places in the right direction—but we did an immense amount of memorizing. There was no learning made easy for us. In grammar we were obliged to recite every word of Murray's large volume over and over, for a long time, before we were set to make practical application of it in the analysis or parsing of a sentence. We must repeat *of, to, for, by, with, in, into, within, without, over, under, through, above, below, before, behind, beneath, on* or *upon, among, after, about, against,* for months before we were permitted to tell what should be done with the smallest preposition of them all.

I remember when at twelve years of age I had recited *Murray's Grammar* through perhaps over a dozen times without a word of explanation or application from the book or the teacher, the master, as I was passing by him to my seat, handed me an open book, and pointing to a passage, said I might study that for a parsing lesson. Alas! it was no open book to me. The sentences which he indicated read: "Dissimulation in youth is the forerunner of perfidy in old age. Its first appearance is a token of growing depravity and future shame." I knew every rule in the grammar but I did not know how to apply one of them even to the first word. I carried the book out at recess, and a more advanced pupil gave me a clue. I put my memory in harness, and soon learned to apply the rules, of which hitherto I had no comprehension.

Still, for that time it was a good school, for we had to work out our own salvation by hard study. The master carried all the time in his hand, a ruler with a leather strap nailed over each end. If he caught an eye wandering from the book, or if he saw signs of restlessness or heard a whisper, he gave the offender a smart blow, particularly if it happened to be his own little motherless boy to whom he was especially cruel.

Our curriculum was narrow but we made good readers and spellers, and those of us who had the gift, good writers, and we were well grounded in grammar.

We were taught our religion in the old Quaker Meeting House—where the seats were hard benches, and where the great beams and rafters had no paint. I think there was no plastering except overhead.

The dear old meeting house was to me an object of great reverence. Our Ministers were two women. I remember one spring day when one of them invited a company of the young girls to go with her to clean the meeting house, we had a jolly time scrubbing the benches and the floors, while she, one of our preachers, white-washed the ceiling and made the occasion as pleasant for us as a picnic. The old house has been destroyed by fire and a more modern structure put in its place. But the old one was a sacred place to me.

I was taken regularly to Meeting, where I was early impressed with the very great blessing of a birthright membership in the Society of Friends; and whatever this may now have become. I do think that at that time and in our circumstances it was a privilege to be thankful for. The preaching we heard was of an emotional character, with very little of the theological; and the moral atmosphere which surrounded us was good. My father and mother were especially diligent in teaching us morally, making good conduct the aim and purpose as well as the test of religious character. My mother was a very modest, quiet, unassuming woman, devoting herself exclusively to her family duties, and she was the most thoroughly honest and truthful woman I ever saw. I have no reason to think she would have varied from the truth in the slightest manner, to save her life. So, whatever of truthfulness and love of the truth have been mine, I attribute to my early training.

After attending Meeting on First Day morning, the afternoon was usually spent in paying or receiving visits, especially in going to our grandfather's. It was not necessary to be invited or to announce our coming—whoever stayed at home expected company. No one objected to sewing or knitting on First Day. Unnecessary housework was avoided. It was against our principles to regard one day as holier than another, but this day was regarded as the day to put on our best apparel, and to be made after our morning meeting a day of recreation.

In these customs of life there grew up in this rural village and its outskirts a group of intelligent thoughtful well-behaved boys and girls, who, at the time of which I write, were just emerging from childhood into manhood and womanhood. Their morality was of a high standard. They were, like their parents, readers and thinkers. I remember well that at our social gatherings, for we had such by ourselves, these boys and girls used to discuss affairs of state as did our parents and their neighbors. We had our rival candidates for office, although we were mostly of one party.

The generation of young people who had preceded us used in their evening parties to play the old fashioned games in which kissing between the boys and girls played a prominent part. We never played them. We were too dignified for that.

The Quaker element among us excluded music. So, instead of singing we recited poetry. It was not uncommon for us to commit

long poems to memory, so we never lacked material for this purpose. Instead of dancing, we played Blind Man's Buff, Puss-in-the-
Corner, and Fox and Geese. We took long walks, jumped the rope,
and rode horseback. Those of us who were Quakers wore the Quaker
costume, addressed all persons by their Christian names, called the
days of the week and the months by their numbers instead of by
what we considered their heathenish names, and we used the singular personal pronouns as *thee* and *thou* and *thy*.

The formal way of addressing a comparative stranger or an old
person among many Quakers is to use both Christian and surname,
but not even this ceremony in address was used among us at the
beginning of the nineteenth century.

At our evening parties to which we sometimes walked two miles,
we had for refreshments fruit or nuts or both, and often cake and
light wine. Total abstinence had not been thought of at that time,
but I remember that when I was fourteen years old, I found that
when I drank the wine it made me dizzy and I renounced it without
ever thinking or hearing that there was any moral harm in it. Cider
was the family dinner drink and I renounced that for the same reason.

The boys and girls walked together going to these parties and
returning from them; and the gatherings ended at nine o'clock.

We had our little partialities and preferences and our youthful
love affairs, but curiously enough not one of them in that group of
boys and girls terminated in matrimony. Perhaps there were too
many cousins among us.

We had great freedom in our set of young people, but our parents were strict about our association with strangers.

A young doctor came to live and practice in our village, and
went about socially, chiefly among the set of girls older than we
were. One day I was standing on a terrace between our dooryard
and that of our next door neighbor, chatting with the neighbor's
daughter, when the doctor came along and stood just below me.
He reached up, took hold of my hands and pulled until I was compelled to jump down. My father happened to be at a window and
saw the performance and when I went in he rebuked me severely
for allowing such a liberty, although I was not really to blame for it.

Two young men who were brothers came to our village and
opened an evening writing school. My sister Lucy and I attended.

As far as appeared they were well-behaved young persons. One evening one of them called at our home and spent an hour or so in the family room. After he went away our father, Arnold Buffum, requested us to give no encouragement to such visits.

About the year 1825 a new schoolmaster came to our village to teach in the Academy. He was George D. Prentice, then just graduated from Brown University, a young man who was afterward distinguished as a lawyer and statesman, and who was for forty years, 1830 to 1870, the brilliant editor of the *Louisville Courier-Journal*, in which he battled royally for the Federal Union, as his state began to be disturbed by the spirit of rebellion which culminated in the Civil War.

Up to the time of his coming to us we had been accustomed to the reading of such books as were in our own library, which was large for that time. It contained only one novel—Hannah Moore's *Coelebs in Search of a Wife*. We also read the books which were to be found in the village library—where were Miss Birney's novels and I think a few others which we were not forbidden to read. We also read the *Spectator* and the *Rambler* and other of Dr. Johnson's writings and the British poets—Milton, Young, Pope, Cowper, Montgomery, and Moore. Also we read especially religious and Quaker books, such as *Barclay's Apology for the People Called Quakers, Piety Promoted, Life of George Fox, Pilgrim's Progress*, and *Works on Female Education*.

Our new schoolmaster soon discovered our literary inclinations and so beside introducing some modern improvements into our school, he helped us in the cultivation of our taste for reading. He taught school every other Seventh Day, and on the alternate Seventh Days he would start in the morning and walk to Providence, fourteen miles, go to Brown University Library, get a number of books, tie them up in a large bandanna handkerchief, bring them home and distribute them among us to be read and be changed about for the next fortnight, then to be returned in the same way and another batch brought out for our delectation. Thus we read the Waverley novels as they were issued from the press, when the author was the "Great Unknown." We had also Scott's and Byron's poems, Cooper's novels, and perhaps some others which I have forgotten.

As Mr. Prentice was our schoolmaster, our parents trusted to his judgment in the choice of books, more than might have been expected, but I remember one day our father took up Byron's *Manfred*, and seeing something in it objectionable, inquired where it came from. On learning that Mr. Prentice brought it to my sisters and me, he walked out of the house with it in his hand and with consternation we saw him enter the house where the master boarded. He returned soon without the book, but as we heard no report of the interview our fears of a general interdict were allayed, and we went on enriching our minds with the new literature.

As it was with the books, so it was with the young man himself; being our teacher he was admitted into our social circle without restraint or question. Since he was not our cousin and was a little older than the boys that were, he became quite a favorite, and was a great addition to our social life.

But alas! when he had been with us a year he declared himself in love with one of my cousins, the loveliest girl in the village, in language so violent and determined, that he was refused by her parents with contumely and disdain. He left town in a state of burning indignation, leaving behind him in the girl an aching heart but a very submissive spirit.

He came back once to attend the wedding of Otis Bartlett and had a glimpse of her in the Friends Meeting and wrote some lines about her containing a reference to this sight of her: "I saw thee in the House of Prayer."

Our religious society forbade the marriage of members with persons not in our fold. The poor girl was sent away to boarding-school, forbidden to answer his letters, which he would write to her, but which we had reason to believe were usually intercepted so that she seldom received them. It was a sad ending to what had been to us a year of much pleasure as well as of lasting benefit.

During one of the later years of my life in the old village a few of the girls of our circle organized a society which we called "The Female Mutual Improvement Society." We agreed to meet one evening in every week and read some useful book, and contribute original compositions of our own.

I do not remember that we had any written constitution, or any officers except a clerk. I do not think any records were preserved, but while the Society lasted we were faithful to our pledges, and we enjoyed the meetings very much.

We had no boys in it; we did not know that we were starting a movement which should spread over the country in a great Federation of Women's Clubs, but we were.

This was many years before the agitation for the immediate emancipation of slaves began, or the prejudice against color was weakened; but my oldest sister Sarah wrote a paper which she dated in the twentieth century in which she pictured the Negroes as in possession of the government and at the head of society; and she stated in it that great consternation existed at the capital because the daughter of the President of the United States had married a white man! I think some of our members did not like the paper very well; but Sarah lived to do valiant service long afterwards as the wife of Nathaniel B. Borden of Fall River, Massachusetts, in the Anti-Slavery Movement and the protection of fugitive slaves.

I think I was, at this time, fifteen years old, and I remember writing an earnest appeal to young girls to seek the improvement of their minds in order to prepare for usefulness in life, and ending with these words, "Remembering that the talent hidden in a napkin obtained not for its owner the answer of 'Well Done.'"

I made a visit soon after that at my uncle's in Providence, and carrying my composition with me, I read it to some boy cousins. Horace Buffum, taking it in his hands, refused to return it to me, and without my knowledge or consent, carried it to the office of the *Manufacturers' and Farmers' Journal.* It was published there, the editor, William E. Richmond, thanking the writer and requesting further contributions. The composition was signed "Anna." It was many years before I complied with this request, but we kept up our Mutual Improvement Association, until we began to be scattered.

We girls were serious minded in those days. One of my letters to my cousin, Eliza Earle at Leicester, Massachusetts, came to my attention not long ago. I was fifteen when I wrote it. "What can be nobler, more refined than a virtuous friendship? Founded on the never failing basis of Virtue and her handmaid Sincerity, it inspires and purifies the heart, raises it above the trifles of the world, and soothes into placid slumber the corroding cares which ofttimes disturb the peace of a feeling mind."

And another at about the same time. "In little villages like our dear Woonsocket, detraction is much too common. I am convinced it is an evil practice. Our sex have long been noted for their fondness for scandal or, as it is sometimes called, tea table talk; but I think there might be exceptions. Do let us, dear Eliza, in our progress through life, show to the world two such exceptions; and while we are securing to ourselves the approbation of others, we shall contribute to our own happiness."

We Buffum girls were very fond of our Earle cousins and corresponded frequently, generally sending our missives by the hand of some accommodating friend who happened to be going to Leicester or from Leicester to Smithfield—this to save postage.

As I compare the manners and people of that time with those of today, in the same station of life, I think that my grandparents, my uncles and aunts and neighhors were most of them persons of strong mental and moral individuality and yet were narrow in their ideas in some directions.

In this day of associated charities, it seems strange that they had no more sympathy with poverty and destitution, no idea of lifting up those lowlier than themselves, and in some cases permitted real neglect of conditions which now we should feel bound to ameliorate. There was a deaf and dumb woman whose home was at the town poor house, several miles from our village. She used to come there occasionally and in her way proclaim her woes in the street. She wore always a very short skirt and a short gown, which we should call now a sack, and she was barefooted. She had short hair and wore no bonnet. She stood on the street and by throwing her arms about she told the crowds which listened to her inarticulate cries, how either the overseer or the keeper had beaten and abused her. We children pitied her, but nobody appeared to do anything for her. Her name was Patience, but we always called her "Deef Pashe." She seemed to be utterly an outcast. I remember one day a vagrant man such as we should now call a "tramp" came along and begged for food, and one of our tavern keepers, hunting up an old Rhode Island law, went out with a horse whip and drove him out of the village. But I do remember that my father came in and spoke of the affair with great indignation, and said it was a shame and an unjustifiable outrage. But the general feeling was that poor people must look out for themselves, that their poverty was their own fault.

In families the husband and father was the person not only to be held in the highest respect, but to be regarded with awe and a kind of fear by all the women.

My mother who was Rebecca Gould of Newport and in whose family there had been more freedom, noticed when she first came into my father's family, that even the married daughters when visiting their parents, if they were chatting with their mother and with each other, always subsided into silence when their father came into the room—he, my grandfather, being regarded as a sort of God-like personage before whom no everyday feminine talk was to be indulged.

Yet there was handed down a story that proved that his own daughters did sometimes beard this lion in his den.

On one occasion, after the eldest daughter Patience had been married to Pliny Earle and had gone to live in Leicester, and the younger two were little girls, my grandfather and grandmother went away for a little visit, leaving Hannah and Lucy, two lively maidens in their teens, as housekeepers. They decided to have a party. They had the wind pipes of some chickens which they had dried for such a purpose. They moulded some candles, putting the wind pipes filled with gunpowder along the sides of the wicks. Then they invited their friends, had a nice supper, the table well lighted with candles. While the supper was going on there was an explosion—everybody was startled but no one was hurt, and the fun was very much enjoyed.

When the father and mother came home, everything had been cleared away and nothing was said. But somehow it got told outside, and the Overseers of the Monthly Meeting of the Quaker Society heard of it, and came to the house to visit the parents of these wild young maidens. Now these parents were very dignified and highly responsible members of the Society. And it was a great mortification to them to be reproved for any disorderly conduct in their own home. So when the Overseers were gone the father summoned the girls into the sitting room and demanded to know what this all meant. When the affair was confessed and explained, he, walking up and down the room, reproved them very severely for such disgraceful conduct. Finally Lucy, who I think was the bolder of the two, said, "Well, I'm very sorry." "Sorry for what?" cried the indignant father, as he stopped before her. "Sorry that thee has found it out," she replied.

Hannah later married, in 1800, William Arnold, and Lucy, also in 1800, Walter Allen.

It was not uncommon for families in this part of the state to take insane persons to board. So far as I remember no harm ever came to anyone from this practice. The insane boarders whom I can recall all seemed happy as well as harmless, except one man. There was a woman who lived thus in one household for twenty years. We used to see her when we visited there, as she moved freely about the house and sat with the family. She never spoke to us, but waved her hands much of the time and appeared to be talking happily to unseen friends, visions floating about her in the air. The man to whom I have referred, on the contrary seemed always troubled. He acted as if he were struggling with an antagonist and striking at somebody. Rumor said that he had been engaged in the slave trade, and those who saw him believed that he was enacting again some old and dreadful scene upon the slave ship.

In those days there used to be a great deal of what was called typhus fever in this neighborhood every autumn. Elderly women were employed as nurses in obstetric cases, but except for these occasions nursing as a profession was unknown. The women in families took care of their own sick by day and depended on their neighbors for watchers at night. I began to go out "watching" when I was fourteen years old. We girls often went, two of us together, on such service. We had a good supper spread for us to eat in the night, and very sick patients were often left to our unskillful care. Our physician was of the old-fashioned, heroic kind. He was somewhat addicted to excessive drinking, and between him and us I fear that too many of our people were laid in untimely graves.

As population increased new industries were added to those of farming and the home utilization of farm products. A hat manufactory was opened near my grandfather's, and a scythe-making establishment, and whetstones were made at a place still further down the road.

The movement towards mill manufacture led to the establishment of small factories for the spinning of cotton yarn. William Buffum and his youngest son William Jr. then became cotton manufacturers. Women from the poorer families used to take bundles of yarn to weave at home into sheetings and shirtings, returning when their tasks were finished to receive their pay in groceries, dry goods, and other articles, including, I am sorry to say, West India rum and Holland gin. My grandfather had a storehouse and could, therefore, advantageously make these payments of "truck" wages. A dye house was operated on his farm and yarns were there dyed in different colors before they were woven into ginghams.

When I was a child some "Old Country men," as we called them, came into our community and offered their services to teach the daughters of farmers some fancy weaving. A few of these strangers were admitted into the families but among the best people it was considered a dangerous experiment thus to receive them, as they had necessarily to be placed in intimate relations with the daughters, and in one or two cases where it was tried there followed very sad consequences.

Power looms, that is, looms operated by water power, were introduced into this country while I was still quite young, and they revolutionized the whole cotton industry in Rhode Island. Young women who had been schoolteachers or tailoresses or who had lived at home dependent on their parents flocked to the growing factory villages, and, like the Lowell Offering, girls carried on literary work while earning such wages as they had never dreamed of. Sometimes they were thus enabled to pay off mortgages on the farms belonging to their fathers, or to add many comforts to the lives of their mothers. Many such girls came into villages near our community, and some of them married and helped to found some of the best families in Rhode Island.

I remember the first American-made calico which was brought home from the factory in our neighborhood. My grandfather gave me two dress patterns of it. The making of presents was less common then than it is now.

A bitter feeling against the mother country still existed in New England in my childhood and pervaded the Buffum household. Near the beginning of the nineteenth century only the youngest son William and daughter Lydia remained unmarried under the paternal roof. A young Englishman, apparently of fine character, came to Massachusetts and built up a manufacturing business. He was a Quaker and made some attempts to win this daughter, but

he was an "Old Country man," and my grandfather discouraged
his advances solely on this account, and he had to obtain a wife
elsewhere. Lydia later, in 1818, married Samuel Shove.

Years after the English lover was sent away from the daughter,
William Buffum's youngest son, William, married Ann L. Sheldon
whose parents were English, and who was born just after they arrived
in this country. She was left an orphan in her youth and became a
governess in the family of John Slater, who founded the Slatersville
Manufacturing company. She attended a Quaker meeting on one
occasion and heard a Quaker sermon, and she was so impressed by
the beauty and spirituality of the faith inculcated therein that she
was converted and joined the Society of Friends. She used the Quaker
language, put on the Quaker costume and habitually walked two
miles every First Day to the meeting house in Union Village. She
captivated my young uncle, married him, and in due time became
the mistress of the colonial homestead. She was a very refined and
elegant woman, handsome, with dark hair and fair skin. Their two
daughters are Anne Vernon Buffum and Mary Lee Buffum, both
living today.

She knew little about her parents, but had reason to believe that
her mother had heen connected with the English aristocracy, and
that the marriage with her father had separated her mother entirely
from her kindred. At the time my uncle married this English girl my
grandfather had become an old man. Perhaps his prejudices had
grown weaker, so that he did not refuse his consent. Moreover, the
parental authority was never exerted so strongly over sons as over
daughters.

My own father in later years consented to my sister Lucy's marriage to the Reverend Nehemiah G. Lovell, a Baptist minister.

My uncle, William, inherited all his mother's sweetness of disposition, and in my childhood I was especially fond of him. His
wedding in the Friends' meeting house was the first one I ever
attended, and to it I wore my first pair of kid gloves.

The ceremony was the ordinary one used by Friends, and it
made a lasting impression on my mind. We went to a week day
morning meeting as for the usual worship. The bridal couple sat
together on a raised seat facing the congregation. Near the time
when the meeting should close, one of the Friends, a member of

a committee already appointed to take charge of the ceremony, requested the pair "to proceed with the business." The bride and groom arose and took each other by the hand. He spoke first saying, "In the presence of this assembly I take this, my friend, Ann L. Sheldon, to be my wife, promising, through Divine assistance, to be unto her a true and affectionate husband until by death we are separated." Still clasping hands, she then said, "In the presence of this assembly I take this, my friend, William Buffum, to be my husband, promising, through Divine assistance, to be unto him a true and affectionate wife until by death we are separated."

A certificate prepared beforehand was then signed by the couple, "she, after the custom of marriage, adopting the name of her husband." All other persons present were next invited to sign their names as witnesses, and then the document was read aloud to the meeting by one of the Friends. The whole scene was beautiful and calculated to emphasize in all minds the sense of responsibility and moral obligation pertaining to married life.

The bride wore for her wedding dress a gown of rich white satin and a neat white silk bonnet. There was no trimming of any kind about her costume, no bows of ribbon and not even buttons. After the marriage the guests were received at the house where she had been making her home, which happened to be that of one of my aunts, one of the groom's married sisters. A few days later the young couple went to his father's and my grandmother gradually gave up the housekeeping to the new daughter, and after the death of the mother the English stranger became the mistress of the colonial homestead.

The *Discipline* of the Society of Friends enjoined very careful oversight of young persons. When a young man or woman moved from the jurisdiction of one Monthly Meeting to another, the certificate of membership which he or she took to the new meeting declared whether such person were or were not under marriage engagements. It was a "disownable" offense for a Friend to marry anyone who did not belong to the Society.

Perhaps the spirit of Quakerism towards the family relation and the institution of marriage can be best understood by a perusal of some passages from the *Book of Discipline* adopted by the New England Yearly Meeting. It is not a common book, and I quote from a volume printed in New Bedford, "by direction of the meeting," in 1809, about eight years before my uncle's marriage:

"It is advised that parents exercise a religious care in watching over their children and endeavor to guard them against improper or unequal connections in marriage; that they be not anxious to obtain for them large portions and settlements, that they be joined with persons of religious inclinations, suitable dispositions and diligence in their business, which are necessary to a comfortable life in a married state.

"And it is particularly recommended to all parents, to endeavor to cultivate such habits of confidence and freedom in the truth with their children as may render it easy for them early to consult their parents in such important concerns.

"It is advised, that all young and unmarried persons in membership with us, previously to their making any procedure in order to marriage, do seriously and humbly wait upon the Lord for His counsel and direction in this important concern, and when favored with satisfactory clearness therein, they should early acquaint their parents or guardians with their intentions, and wait for their consent; thus preservation from the dangerous bias of forward, brittle and uncertain affections would be experienced, to the real benefit of the parties, and the comfort of their friends.

"It is agreed, that no Monthly Meeting permit any marriages to be proposed in said Meeting, sooner than one year after the decease of former husband or wife; and we think it most advisable, that no such proposals be made between the parties, within that time.

"For the accomplishment of marriage, it is advised, that the parties should inform the men's and women's Monthly Meeting to which the woman belongs of their intentions, through the Preparative Meeting when convenient. And at a proper time they should make it known in both meetings, either by a written communication signed by both parties or by a verbal declaration, that, 'with divine permission and Friends' approbation, they intend marriage with one another,' whereupon two Friends in each meeting (if both parties belong to the same meeting) should be appointed to make the necessary inquiries respecting the clearness to proceed in marriage, of the party or parties who shall be members of said Monthly Meeting.

"If the parties have parents or guardians present, their consent should be expressed; or if the man is a member of another Monthly Meeting, the consent of his parents or guardians, if he have any, should be produced in writing with a certificate from his Monthly Meeting, of his clearness, either then or at the next meeting.

"If the woman be a widow, having children, two or more friends should be appointed to see that the rights of her children are legally secured. At the next meeting the committee report that careful inquiry has been made and that they have the consent of parents, where it has not before been manifested, and the parties appear clear to proceed in marriage with each other, the meeting is to leave them at liberty to accomplish their marriage according to our rules and to appoint two Friends of each sex, to attend and see that good order is observed, that a certificate be prepared, and after being signed by the parties at their marriage be audibly read, and that a sufficient number of witnesses be thereto subscribed.

"It is further advised, that the said marriage be accomplished decently, gravely and weightily; and that the parties themselves, and others concerned, do take care at the houses or places where they go after the marriage is over, that all behave with becoming sobriety; and that the paid Overseers are to make report to the next Monthly Meeting, and take care that the marriage certificate be recorded."

The *Discipline* also advises, "That such men and women Friends as do make suit or concern themselves in proposals of marriage, one to the other, do not dwell in the same house, from the time they begin to be concerned, until their marriage."

I think there was, up and down the country road that ran through the village and by the farms whose people I knew in my childhood, a large amount of happy home life, and much intelligence and real comfort. If there was less for women to do outside their homes, there was more work in them. They were skilled in all the methods of using the needle, and the overseaming, the hemming, the felling, the stitching and hemstitching, the buttonholing and quilting, the over-casting, running, and darning that was done would appall the women of today. Colleges and high schools were not open to the girls, who nevertheless improved such opportunities as they had. In my family we used to have much reading aloud in the evenings, and I think more effort was made in the schools then than now to train the pupils to be good readers.

In all this community there seemed to be a growing desire among the men to introduce into their homes improvements which would make life easier for the women. Cooking stoves were first used about the year 1818, clothes posts and clothes lines at nearly the same time. Before then the clothes that had been washed were dried on bushes and on the grass.

There were indeed in the families whom I knew some cases of married unhappiness, but I never knew of a divorce among all the descendants of Joseph and Margaret Buffum during the first third of this century, or an instance of pauperism or crime.

During the years included in these reminiscences we were under the old common law as it had come to us from our English ancestry by which married women had no property rights. Whatever they had inherited or earned by their own labor be-came on their marriage the property of their husbands. When a rich girl married it was often said that "she brought her husband a handsome fortune." Although many of the older women whom I then knew were interested in political affairs, it never seemed to trouble them that they had no share in the management of the subjects of their interest. The home cares satisfied them, and the idea of woman suffrage had not entered the Rhode Island mind.

My father, Arnold Buffum, became very much interested dur-ing my childhood in sheep raising. A finer breed of sheep than we had before had in this country was imported from Spain at about that time, and he used to buy and sell them. Whenever he heard that any farmer had one or more of these sheep, he would go to see him in the way of business. Much of his traveling on these errands was done by driving in some sort of private vehicle. He sometimes took me with him, and on one of these excursions

I had an experience which illustrated to me the difference between the religious toleration in Rhode Island, which permitted an easy observance of the Sabbath, and the stricter habits and thought in other states. Our journey on this occasion brought us on a First Day morning to the entrance of a Connecticut village. My father, I dare say, was repeating texts of scripture or passages of religious poetry, as was his wont, when a tall, stern-looking, middle-aged man came rushing hatless out of his house and beckoned us to stop.

As we obeyed he exclaimed, "By virtue of my authority as a magistrate of this town, I forbid your driving here on the Lord's Day."

My father courteously and calmly explained our circumstances and the inconvenience it would be to us to spend the day in a tavern, for he did not offer us the hospitality of his house, and finally he allowed us to proceed. We passed the village church and my father pointed out to me the whipping post in front of it, and we had reason to be thankful that the Blue Laws were not then in force.

In the early part of the century the people were infected with the fever for going West to seek new homes. They spoke of "going to the Ohio." The Ohio then represented to their imaginations the farthest western limit of habitable land. I do not think that many persons really went from our vicinity, but they loved to talk about going and to try to think what life would be like if they should take the long wagon journey and leave everything that they had ever known behind them.

When I was seventeen years old I went to the Friends Boarding School in Providence, others of our circle doing the same. While I was there my family left Smithfield and moved to Fall River, Massachusetts, to my very great grief. My life there however turned out to be almost as happy and it was in Fall River that I later met and married my dear husband, Samuel G. Chace.

Since then I have only returned to the dear old Smithfield house as a visitor, but to this day the place is to me the "spot of earth supremely blest—a dearer sweeter spot than all the rest."

And now in 1897 in the ninety-first year of my age, as I have recalled to memory these annals of my early life, every now and then some item, a little indistinct, has made me wish to inquire of some one for information, and then I have recollected that not one of that group of hoys and girls of my age in Smithfield is left upon the earth, except myself.

• 2 •

Some Recollections
of Her Girlhood

by Lydia Buffum Read,
Written in 1892

I was eight years old when I came to live in Fall River with my father and mother and two older sisters and younger brothers, leaving by two eldest sisters to come by stagecoach afterwards.

Moving time is always a happy time for children, but ours was very pleasant, for it presented so many delightful changes; and when we came to Slade's Ferry our rapture knew no bounds. William Slade and his hired man ferried us across and we went up Main Street to the Four Corners to a hotel called the "Sign of the Golden Eagle," ostensibly kept by Bradford Durfer, but really kept by his wife and her three daughters; and a very good house it was, too.

The next day our furniture arrived, and we went to housekeeping in a house which stood on the ground where the new courthouse now stands, and which was afterwards burned. I used to stand by our front gate, where I could see the spire of the only steeple house in Fall River at that time.

Oh, how happy it made me. It was like painting and poetry but Fall River was only a village in the town of Troy then. It had only a few meeting houses and these of simple unpretentious type. This one that I loved to look at was the First Congregational Church, and answered for them until they built the stone church. No sect had more than one meeting house. We were members of the Society of Friends, and early found our place in that meeting.

There was a large old-fashioned-looking house that stood half in Massachusetts, and half in Rhode Island, built by general subscription, and used by all when needed as a meeting house. I went there one evening to hear Lucretia Mott with a relative who was visiting us, but we found the house full and could get no further than the steps. We looked in at the windows, and we could see her beautiful face and hear her impassioned voice, but not connected enough to understand, so we soon went home. The place on which this house stood was afterward taken into Massachusetts.

There was no kindergarten or public school in Fall River, and I doubt if any in that part of the country, and my two eldest sisters started an infant school in a home owned by Mr. N. B. Borden, and located near his dwelling house. I was the little girl to assist them, and we had a great many scholars, but the price was very small.

In another year the house was wanted for a public school, and my sisters were asked to be assistant teachers, and I was a scholar, as our infant school was given up. I remember very few of the names of those children, but one stands in my memory very distinctly. When asked what his name was he always answered, "Bitten Hull." His mother always came in the morning with him, so proud and happy in her boy, and well she might be, for we all loved him.

Back of our house was a very steep and high hill, and in the winter, when covered with snow or ice, it made a very good sliding place for us, and we went down on boards, for we had no sleds. I would not dare to risk my neck now in such a way, but we were not a bit afraid and never got hurt.

One evening we had a young girl who had been spending the day with us and we were going part way home with her, the ground on the east side of us was an apple orchard, and very thick. On the west side sloping toward the river it was springy and wet, and as we stood talking with her before parting I saw over the wall a ball apparently of fire moving right out of the orchard, clear the stone wall, then slide across the street, and then disappear on the wall on the other side. It was just about the size of the melons which the farmers raise now. I had read about it and knew it was the "will-o'-the-wisp."

Rock Street was the street east of Main that had my house built on it. Above that street we found a large flat rock thickly surrounded with trees. My sister decided it was just the place to give Hannah More's *Search After Happiness*. I was one of the little girls in that play, and we acted before a very select company of invited guests, much to their satisfaction.

In the society there were a few young men and we had our reading society and once in a while a clambake. I joined an excursion of our young people to Mount Hope. The young men hired a sloop and Jervis Shore acted as captain. The rest fell into line and assisted him. We went to King Philips Retreat, where we drank of his spring water, then climbed the mount and sat in his armchair, visited the old red farmhouse and made ourselves happy. Jervis Shore was very fond of reading, was scholarly and kind hearted. He would rejoice in the improvements in public schools and libraries.

Nursing was not done as a business when I was a young girl. People took care of their sick friends in the day time, and depended on their neighbors to come in and watch with them nights and I did my full share, not only with those I knew, but with those I did not. I remember going with a lady friend into the neighborhood to take care of a young woman, the mother of three little children. She was a very sick woman, and we spent a dreary night. There was one nurse I remember, who was a perfect blessing where she went. She would do anything wanted of her, and for the first four weeks charged two dollars a week. If she stayed longer her price was a dollar and a half. I never saw her faithfulness exceeded. Of doctors we had few, though one stands out in my memory as a good conscientious man. Doctor Thomas Wilbour, a man who remonstrated when the other doctors doubled their prices on office calls and house calls and raised confinement cases from three to five dollars. He said the first price was enough.

In the infant school we formed our first anti-slavery society. We women and girls determined that every woman in the place should have a chance to petition congress to abolish slavery in the District of Columbia and the territories, and what a sight of ignorance we found, many thinking there were no slaves in the country. We found it easier to get those who had intelligence to sign our petition. We were never mobbed but sometimes we had threats.

At this time there were no drinking saloons in the place, though we suspected there were some of the grocers who kept it. There was not a Catholic church nor an Irish person and only one woman, American, who went out to work by the day. I cannot recall her name, but she was very smart, both with her tongue and hands. When she had saved a little money, she employed some men to build her a small home and she took hold with her own hands and helped them. She told me that some of the meeting folks told her she would go to destruction when she died, but she believed she had done too much work in her life for God to allow her to be lost. I never knew or heard of her doing a wrong thing.

About this time the public school first became agitated by the report that the world was coming to an end and the day and hour was fixed. I must confess that it had a good deal of effect on my own mind. On passing John Collon's store I heard some men discussing this matter, and one man said, "When a man dies the world comes to an end with him." That was a comfort to my mind.

• 3 •

Diary Exerpts

by Lucy Buffum Lovell,
1840–1843

October 15, 1840

We have recently lost our baby Laura, and we thought, my husband Nehemiah and I, that little Caroline would some day like to read of her dear little sister's short but happy life, and about her all too early departure to that far better world. I will try to record here the story of Caroline's babyhood as well as Laura's.

Caroline Brooks Lovell, our first child, was born in Amherst, Massachusetts, on January 8, 1837. Her father was pastor of the Baptist Church there, and we lived in Amherst until 1839, when we removed to live with my sister Elizabeth Chace, in Pawtucket. We stayed with her until 1840, at which time my husband was called to the Baptist Church in Bellingham, Massachusetts.

Caroline was a very feeble child, when first born, and weighed, with a good deal of clothing on, four pounds eleven ounces. She

took a severe cold the second week, while I was endeavoring to get
her to nursing, and had a fit which alarmed us very much. We had
scarcely any hope from the first that she would live, and after this
we had still less. Her cold seemed to be settling on her lungs, and
we thought would certainly carry her off. But her life was spared
and she grew stronger, and, though very slowly, increased in size.
At the age of thirteen months she had the scarlet fever. We thought
her dangerously sick and feared the brain would be affected. But
she still was spared. About the time of her recovery it was thought
best for me to wean her. I did so, and the same day she was attacked
with a bilious fever which lasted perhaps a fortnight. This was in
February 1838. When she was three months old she weighed nine
and three-quarter pounds; at the age of fifteen months, fifteen
pounds. The next summer we took her with us to Fall River. The
journey, change of diet, and teething during the hottest part of the
year, in the month of July, brought on a very severe attack of summer complaint, which continued nearly all summer. I ought to have
said before, that, when well, she seemed generally very happy, though
of a nervous temperament, and very easily excited. She would sit on
the floor and play with her blocks or spools in a room by herself, if
I was engaged in another room, perhaps an hour at a time. If I came
and looked in upon her pleasantly employed, with her play, I would
say, "Happy baby," and leave her. She soon caught the sound, and
would say it over two or three times in succession, "Appy baby,
appy baby," apparently from a consciousness of happiness.

At the time I was speaking of when she was so sick, we feared we
should never get her home again. As soon as we thought she was able to
endure the journey, we started for home. The day was excessively warm
but we rode as far as Smithfield, and spent the night with Uncle William
Arnold. Caroline seemed to grow more feeble, until we arrived at Amherst
on Saturday and called our physician, who cut her gums, and left some
medicine which seemed to benefit her. In a few weeks after our return
whortleberries were ripe. I gave her one or two, and finding she was very
fond of them, I gave her a few more, and as those did not seem to hurt
her, I continued to increase her allowance, and in a few days I allowed
her to eat freely of them. She seemed to enjoy them very much, and I
attributed her restoration to health, in a great measure at least, to those
berries. Other summer fruits we felt obliged to deny her. When winter

came we allowed her apples, very freely, and they appeared to do her good. She gained flesh, and appeared remarkably well for a month or two. In November of this year of 1838 her father left home on a mission for the church, and, just before he left, Caroline was taken with a bilious fever again. It lasted as before, about a fortnight, and then she seemed to recover as good a state of health as before.

In February of 1839, on the 15th, our dear little Laura Martha was born. She weighed five pounds eleven ounces, just one pound more than Caroline did at first, and seemed to be a healthy child. When Caroline first saw her she seemed to be filled with astonishment and for several minutes could only exclaim, "Why! Why! Why!" When allowed to kiss her, she seemed perfectly happy. As Laura grew she became a source of happiness to us all. In the spring, when Laura was three months old, we took them both with us to New York. They endured the journey very well, and we had a pleasant visit, as they had no sickness except what was caused by vaccination.

When Caroline was about a year old it became necessary for me to teach her her first lesson in obedience. The shovel and tongs seemed to fascinate her and she would take them and carry them around the house. I forbade her to touch them. She seemed perfectly to understand me, but continued to get them. I tried various ways to dissuade her from her purpose and finally concluded the best method was to divert her attention to some other object. In this way her desire for these things was at last overcome. But she had yet to learn obedience. When she was nearly two years old she one day took a cushion out of a chair and was bringing it across the room. I told her to carry it back and put it in the chair. She did not obey, and after repeating the requisition several times, to no purpose, I felt obliged to use corporal punishment. She had never before heard of such a thing, and of course knew nothing about it. So that it was some time before I could make her understand that there was any connection between the correction and the fault. But she finally yielded. During all this time she did not seem angry in the least, and indeed I do not know that I have ever seen her so. The next occasion of discipline was a few months after, when she was required to go to bed awake. I found that she recollected the penalty of disobedience and I had only to refer to it to secure compliance with my wishes. From that time she has generally gone to bed alone, without a light, very pleasantly. In February of 1839 we left Amherst and went to Pawtucket to board with my sister Elizabeth Chace. There little Laura spent some happy months gaining the affection of the whole family, particularly her Aunt Elizabeth Chace. She was just at an age to be most docile and lovely. Once or twice I had to correct her for pulling sister's and cousin's hair. She seemed to understand the object of correction sooner than Caroline and when once she had learned that she must obey, she seemed to understand that it would be useless to resist, or grieve about it.

Early in the spring of 1840, while her father was supplying the church in Sturbridge for a few Sabbaths, Caroline was sick with a violent attack of lung fever. We were able, however, by vomiting her freely, to break it up so that in the course of a week from the time she was taken sick she began to recover, and was, in a few weeks more, restored to health. It was soon after this that I first took particular pains to teach her of the existence and nature of God and of our relation and duty to Him. I took her to the window in the morning when the rising sun was tingeing the clouds with all the colors of the rainbow and told her that our Father in Heaven made all so beautiful. I spoke to her of the goodness of our Father in Heaven, by which name I always called Him when speaking to her, thinking it would give her a more distinct and favorable, as well as correct, idea of an unseen Being, than the name of God could convey. But I found that she very soon used the one for the other. I frequently took her into my chamber and knelt with her in prayer. But she seemed to take no particular interest in it at that time.

I said very little to her of death, wishing to wait until she could understand something of it. This I considered very important. Young children, unless very judiciously taught upon this subject, are apt to be terrified at the thought of death, especially when told that sometime they too must die. When she asked me if I had a grandmother and grandfather, and I told her I had not, and when the question followed, had I ever, and then, where they were now, I told her they had died and gone to Heaven to live with God. Her first ideas of death, though of course very indistinct, were, I hope, pleasant.

In April of 1840, my brother William Buffum carried me with the children, to Fall River, to visit their grandfather, Arnold Buffum. The air was rough and cold and I was exposed in nursing Laura, so that I took a severe cold and was taken sick the next morning. Whether Laura took cold on the way or took it wholly from me I do not know, but she was attacked with fever and diarrhea at the same time. I was threatened with lung fever and unable to sit up for nearly a week so that I could have but little care of the children. Laura had always been a very timid child in the presence of strangers and would seldom go to any one until she had lived with them several weeks. She however at this time seemed providentially to be very fond of her grandfather and would even go from me to him. If I had her with me on the bed and she heard her grandfather's voice as he came into the house, she would cry to go to him. He became very much attached to her and would take great pains to amuse her. She was not, until we had been at Fall River more than a week, willing to go to any other member of the family, and if it had not been so ordered that she should like to be with her grandfather, I do not know what I should have done. Her father was then in Bellingham and we did not like to send for him. After I recovered so as to be able to go out, Sister Martha Lovell took care of Laura one Sabbath afternoon while I went to meeting.

Caroline enjoyed this visit very much and was generally a very good child. She slept with her aunts and was willing to go upstairs to bed without me and be left in the dark to go to sleep. She enjoyed very much going on the Sabbath with her grandfather to Aunt Laura Lovell's Infant Sabbath School and on a week day to her Day School. These privileges she remembered a long time and often after our return spoke of them.

I said she was generally good, but once or twice I had some difficulty in enforcing obedience. Once she had a little coffee pot her Aunt Martha Lovell had lent her to play with, and she took a notion to stand on it. I told her she must not stand on it, it would spoil it. She persisted in doing it and at the same time saying, "Daughter don't feel able to stand on the floor." I was obliged to shut her up in the bedroom before I could get her to obey me.

I recovered my health in less than a fortnight. Laura had recovered hers before I did mine. My husband came to take us back to Pawtucket and we had a very pleasant journey home. On the way Caroline saw some lambs and was very much pleased. She exclaimed, while her eyes sparkled with delight, "O, I'm glad, I'm glad." And we felt that we were well paid for all the trouble children caused in journeying, by seeing and sharing in the happiness they enjoyed.

When we reached Pawtucket we found Sister Rebecca Spring there with her dear little boy, and the children were pleased to meet him and their other dear cousin, John Gould Chace. My husband left us in a day or two for Sturbridge again. He was away so much of the time that when he was with us he seemed almost a stranger to Laura and she was unwilling he should take her in his arms.

The next week after we returned from Fall River I weaned Laura. Her Aunt Elizabeth Chace, who loved her very much, staid up in my room with her one day and I staid downstairs. Towards night I went up and took her. She asked to nurse but did not cry much and soon got down on the floor and began to play. She was easily weaned, seeming to understand that she could not nurse again, but from that time for more than a month she would always cry if I left her a moment when she was awake. I attributed this to my leaving her all day when I weaned her, and should never advise any mother to do so.

Soon after Laura was weaned we removed to Bellingham. Laura was very much afraid of every stranger, and even of her father, but in the course of a week became acquainted with him again, and with Elizabeth Yerrinton, a friend, so that I was able to leave her, and go to meeting all day, the first Sabbath after we returned.

Caroline commenced going to meeting after we had been here a few weeks. She did not sit very still, though she did quite as well as we expected.

Caroline and Laura both enjoyed the summer very much. They were out doors a great deal of the time, either walking, or riding in the little wagon. Caroline would frequently go out and gather a bunch of wild flowers and bring them in for her little sister, who would sit on the floor and amuse herself half an hour or more in pulling them to pieces. When we went out to ride, or spend an afternoon, we generally took them with us, and they enjoyed it very much.

In the course of the summer I got Laura so that she would go to sleep in her little crib. Sometimes I had some difficulty with her, but generally when she saw that I was decided, she would go quietly to sleep. She usually took a book in her hand when she went into her crib, and held it fast, till she was asleep, and she looked lovely to the eye of a parent as she lay with her little limbs curled up and her book in her hand. How often we gazed upon her, how often impressed a kiss upon her sweet cheek, as she lay there in sleeping innocence. She began to walk when about eighteen months old. This was a time of interest to us all. Caroline took great delight in enticing her to come to her. She was very fearful to take a step at first, and for several days would fall two or three times in going from one side of the room to the other, but soon became accustomed to it, and would laugh very heartily whenever she fell, and jump up and continue her tottering walk. By degrees her limbs gained strength and she ventured to get out at the door and walk on the ground. She would frequently get her little sun bonnet, and putting it on with the front behind, and cape before, would be out and walking off towards the barn before we missed her from her play in the house.

She was very fond of going up and down stairs even before she could walk. This her Aunt Elizabeth Chace taught her. One day she crept out in the front entry, and it was some time, perhaps ten minutes, before I missed her from my side. I went out to see where she was, and saw nothing of her in the entry. I followed her upstaris and went into my room, the door of which was open, but she was not there. Trembling, I followed on to the store room, the door of which was also open, and found her standing by a meal chest, apparently very much pleased with her exploit. She had passed directly by the head of the back stairs to get into this last room, and I felt that it was a merciful Providence that kept her from falling down these, as well as the ones by which she came up.

About the last of August Laura was taken sick with summer complaint. She had been remarkably well and her bowels seemed to be in a very good state Wednesday morning. I thought particularly of this as many children in neighboring towns, and some in this, were dying with dysentery, and I spoke of it to her father. Before night, however, a diarrhea came on, and we felt some afraid she was going to be sick. But she was very pleasant through the day, and especially at night just before going to bed. She stood up in a chair in which I was sitting by the window and said a good many words that she had never said before. She had before seemed to understand most of our conversation when we spoke to her and would almost invariably answer correctly, "No," or, "Yes," so that we could

carry on quite a conversation with her by asking her questions. But
at this time she seemed to want to say new words, and said "Tow,"
for "cow," and some others which I do not recollect. I asked her to
say, "Mrs. Johnson," she had always called her "Dos" but now she
seemed to make an extra effort, and said "Miss Dos."

About midnight we perceived that she was very feverish and
thought some of calling the physician. But she seemed to sleep pretty
quietly and we thought best to wait till morning. In the morning
the physician came, and cut her gums, which were very much swol-
len, and administered some gentle cathartic. She grew sicker that
day, and the next, so that we had her in her crib down stairs and did
not dress her. After that she slept a great deal for a day or two and
then began to get better. In about a week from the time she was
taken she was able to be dressed. Her appetite returned and gradually her strength, so that she got down on the floor and walked and
even got out at the door herself. We carried her crib upstairs and
she went up there again to sleep in the day time. We had before
taken her up there nights.

While she was sick, especially after she began to get better, she
wanted either her father or mother to stand by her, and as the flies were
very troublesome to her, we would sometimes quiet her by saying,
"Father will keep the flies away," or, "Mother will keep the flies away,"
or "Go away, flies." She became accustomed to the sound, and seemed
to consider it a kind of lullaby. After she got well enough to go up stairs
and have her morning nap, I one day put her in her crib as usual, and
giving her a book, left her to go to sleep. After I had gone out I stopped
in the entry a few moments to listen and see whether she would go
quietly to sleep. Presently she began to make a noise, and I thought she
seemed to be trying to say something. I listened and heard her say
several times very earnestly, "Wa, wi, wa wi." I immediately supposed
she wanted me to come and stay with her, and though there were
scarcely any flies in the chamber, which was kept dark, I supposed she
had taken that measure to get me to come and stay with her. I went in
and said, "Does Laura want mother to keep the flies away?" "Ish, ish,"
said she, and I staid with her, motioning with my hand for the flies to
go away, and she went quietly to sleep.

She continued to gain strength, though her bowels never recovered their healthy tone, and she seemed to enjoy her food, and play,

and to be happy. One morning her father was going to Providence and I took the children in the carriage, after it came to the door, before he was quite ready to start, and rode with them about half a mile. It was a delightful morning in September and Laura seemed to enjoy the ride as much as any of us. It was a placid kind of enjoyment but I well remember the sweet calm expression of her lovely blue eyes.

The next morning, as usual, she had some new milk brought up before she was dressed, and drank nearly half a pint from her little tin cup, and also ate a piece of plain gingerbread. She had always, since she was weaned, been in the habit of eating something when she first woke in the morning. After we came downstairs she drank some more milk. I thought she had a a better appetite than usual, but suppose now that it was thirst, for she very soon lost it all. I perceived she was unwell again and sent for the doctor, but he had gone to Boston. This was on Wednesday, and he did not call till Friday evening. He did not think she was very sick, told me to feed her with simple food and give her a little magnesia. In the morning he called again and cut her gums. Since he had cut them before, three eye teeth had come through the gums. It was the fourth that seemed now to be the cause of her sickness, as I have no doubt her first sickness was caused by the inflammation of the other three. On Sabbath morning she seemed rather more unwell and exceedingly languid and feeble. She would answer when spoken to, but did not seem inclined to talk, or play of her own accord. That day I took off her frock and put on a flannel nightgown, and I never dressed her afterwards.

Monday she continued to grow more feeble, and Monday night her disorder assumed the form of dysentery. Then we began to feel more alarmed. Though the doctor encouraged us, and had it not been coming on so gradually, we should have thought there was nothing particularly alarming in the case. Tuesday we gave her oil, and after it, opium injections, to quiet the bowels—but she grew worse. Tuesday and Wednesday she seemed to suffer a great deal, and though we did not think she would so soon leave us, we felt that we had reason to fear she would not stay long with us. She kept up a moaning noise nearly all the time those two days, and slept but little. I had her in my arms most of the time. She was not willing any one else should hold her, not even her father, so that it was extremely difficult for me to leave a moment. Some of the time when she was worrying, she would sit up erect in my lap, and although so weak, seemed unwilling I should support her at all. If I put my hand to her back, she would put it away. I suppose her flesh was so sore and tender that she could not bear to have one touch her.

We fed her with gum arabic, tapioca, and rice water. She seemed to prefer the last and drank a great deal of it. The doctor prohibited all solid food, but she seemed almost to the last to have a craving for it. We did not dare to let her see any solid food, if she did, she would cry for it. She saw her grandfather take something to eat from the closet one day, and she cried some time on account of it. I took her into the front parlor away from all food so that she might not be distressed by the sight of what she could not have. One day a loaf of bread was brought in from the oven for me to say whether it was done or not. She saw it and cried for it. I think this was on Thursday, the day before she died. Once she cried for some gingerbread she saw Caroline have.

She seemed more comfortable Thursday than the two previous days, and we felt some encouraged, though her medicine did not seem to have a good effect. We gave her laudanum injections, and while the effect lasted, she would sleep. But the irritation of the bowels continued and we were obliged, according to the directions of the physician, to repeat the injections, and increase the dose. We began with about twenty drops of laudanum in a very little starch, and increased the dose till we got it up to fifty drops.

Thursday evening she slept quietly and I felt some encouraged. I partly made up a cap for Mother Lovell, who sat with me in the room with Laura, and felt deeply interested for her. I could not quite finish it, but told her I hoped I should be able to the next evening, as I thought Laura seemed more comfortable and would perhaps be still better the next evening. Little did I then think that we should be called to see her die the next evening.

She seemed very thirsty during the night, and drank, I should think, more than a pint of rice water. In the morning I perceived, about six o'clock, that a change had taken place. Her hands and feet were cold, and she seemed very uneasy. She would lie down a moment in my lap, and then want me to rest her hand on my arm, and seemed to desire constantly to change her position. She began about this time to rub her eyes, nose and mouth, with her fingers, and by noon she had raised large blisters on her lips by rubbing them. During the forenoon she took scarcely any nourishment and seemed very much distressed. She was very restless. I think she did not sleep a moment. She wanted to go from me, and her Grandfather Lovell offered to take her. She had always before refused to go to him, although he had tried hard to get acquainted with her and win her affections. But now she gladly accepted the offer, and from that time while consciousness lasted, seemed to prefer to be with him. He walked about with her and tried to make her as comfortable as she could be. Her grandmother had frequently watched by her crib to keep the flies away, and once when I was out, Laura waked, and wanted to get up. Her grandmother asked her if she should take her, and she said, "Ish," so that her grandmother took her up, and I believe she felt it to be a privilege, as we all did, to do anything for her.

On Friday, while her grandfather had her, I felt very anxious to take her, and after dinner I persuaded him to give her up to me. About one half past two in the afternoon, as I had her in my arms, she seemed to sink into a stupor. Her agitation subsided, she closed her eyes, stretched herself out in my lap, and breathed short and distressed. Her mouth was open and her tongue constantly quivering. I thought she was dying, and would not probably live more than an hour, and I supposed she would die in my arms. I felt anxious to hold her as long as she lived and do what I could for her. But she continued to lie like this, much longer than we expected, so that we concluded she would be more comfortable in her crib, and at the same time that I should have an opportunity to rest some. We moved the crib out into the middle of the room and laid the little sufferer in it. She sometimes had a slight spasm, but most of the time laid in a stupid state.

In the evening the neighbors, a good many of them, came in to weep with us. About one half past seven Laura ceased to breathe for two or three minutes. Her pulse was gone and we thought her spirit had left us. But as we stood weeping round her she gave a deep gasp, then another and another, and then opened her eyes and began to breathe again as before. She then cried in quite a natural voice, and seemed to want something. I went to her and said, "Laura, do you want mother to take you up and give you some drink?" "Ish," she said, in that sweet voice which we used so to love, but which we expected never to hear again. I do not recollect distinctly, but think she extended her hands towards me. I took her once more into my arms. Her father thought then that she might revive and possibly recover, but I did not. We dropped some nourishing liquid into her mouth from a tea spoon, and she swallowed a little. Very soon she began to be distressed again and the doctor administered an opiate, which soon quieted her, and she was laid back in her crib. From this time she seemed to have but little consciousness.

She had during the whole of her sickness been unwilling Dr. Stanley should touch her. She probably remembered his cutting her gums, and she was so extremely sensitive that if he attempted to feel her pulse when she was almost asleep, she would immediately awaken. He scarcely ever had an opportunity of feeling her pulse, and never unless she was sound asleep. But on Friday afternoon and evening she seemed wholly to have lost that sensitiveness. During the evening she remained much as she had been in the afternoon till about one-half past ten, when her breath was suspended again for a few moments. But by raising and rubbing her, it was restored again as before, with the exception that she did not revive as before. She continued to breathe quicker and quicker ten or fifteen minutes, and then without the least struggle, or anything to show that death had done its work, her spirit winged its way to another, better world. Her eyes were sweetly closed by the hand of death, there was no distortion of the muscles, no contraction of the limbs. She was peaceful, and we could scarcely believe that she would not breathe again.

Perhaps it was parents' partiality, but to us Laura seemed an unusually interesting and lovely child. Her temperament was even and her disposition sweet. It seemed to be no cross to her to obey, unless in some particular instances, and then she manifested unusual decision of character. She would resist until she saw there was decision which she could not overcome, and that resistance was useless, and then she would very pleasantly yield. And being once overcome, she seemed to remember the discipline, and seldom would transgress the same way again. Her short life was apparently a very happy one. She had very little sickness until the last. She seemed to enjoy the last summer of her life very much, when she could amuse herself with flowers, or get out and breathe the fresh air. Sometimes she would sit on the carpet half an hour pulling a rose in pieces and scarcely say a word. Indeed her happiness generally was not of a boisterous kind but of that quiet nature which best prepared the mind for the journey of life.

I have thought, if she had lived, there would have been a wide difference between her and Caroline. Hers probably would have been a more even path; perhaps less of enjoyment and less of suffering. But it is useless to conjecture what she would have been, though I find my mind is much inclined either to look back and think what she was to us, or look forward to what she would have been. Better is it for me to think of her as she is—in the arms of Jesus, who said, "Suffer little children to come unto me and forbid them not." Why should we wish to hold her here? True, she was a lovely flower, and we often think how pleasant would our fireside have been this winter if she could have been spared to us. I feel that I could cheerfully make any sacrifice to promote her welfare. O, may I remember that she is where she needs not a mother's watchful care, for the eye of the compassionate Saviour is upon her, and His arms enfold her. She is safe from all the storms of life in the heaven of eternal rest. I shall never feel anxiety on her account lest she should at last lose her soul. And if I, through grace, am admitted to the abode of the Blessed, I shall meet among the happy throng around the throne, my sweet little Laura.

Laura was buried on Sabbath afternoon about five o'clock, September 20, 1840. In the morning Father Shubael Lovell preached from II Cor. 4:17 and 18. "Our light affliction which is but for a moment, worketh for us a far more exceeding and eternal weight of glory." Never did the truth of the Gospel seem more precious. We were led in our minds to look away from things seen and temporal to those which are unseen and eternal.

In the afternoon my husband preached from Job 5:7. "Man is born unto trouble, as the sparks fly upward." I did not go out in the afternoon, but he expressed to me that he felt it a privilege to preach.

Rev. Mr. Smith of Woonsocket came over to attend the funeral. He offered prayer at our house and a few friends were present, after which we went to the meeting house wherein we heard the 103rd Psalm read and remarks by Brother Smith. It was a solemn occasion, and, I hope, led some to reflect more upon eternal things than we are apt to do.

We then, after taking the last look, followed the remains of the little one, beautiful even in death, to the house appointed for all living.

I had told Caroline, the day before, that little sister was dead, that her soul had gone to live with God in Heaven and we must bury her body in the ground. She asked why we must bury it. I told her it would decay if we did not. I endeavored to prepare her mind to part with the beloved object. She hardly knew what death was, but when I took her into the room and let her kiss Laura, she at once exclaimed that her face was cold. We all loved to look upon her while she remained with us. I think I never saw a corpse so lovely and beautiful before, and I felt it was a privilege to be near it and do what I could for it.

Although I had endeavored to prepare Caroline to part with her little sister's remains, yet she had no distinct idea of death and the grave. And when we stood by the open grave, and saw the coffin lowered into it, she screamed as if horror struck, "O Mother, take her up again, take her up again!" She cried, as we turned away from the grave, and continued to do so until we reached home, and I began to regret we had taken her with us to receive such unpleasant ideas of the last resting place of her we loved. I took her upstairs and tried to soothe her agonized spirit. I told her that was dear Laura's little bed. "What," she said, "that deep hole?" "Yes," I said, "they will put green grass over it and in the spring we will plant flowers there, and it will be pleasant, and we shall love to go there and see it." This calmed her agitated spirit, and from that moment she has seemed to think of death only as the way to Heaven, if we are good, and the grave, only as the resting place of the body. I think for several months the death of Laura had a good effect upon Caroline. She seemed more gentle and affectionate, and her mind seemed very much turned to heavenly things, and the study of religion, if I may so express it, was her delight. A new and very wide field of interest was opened to her naturally inquiring mind.

She asked one evening after she had gone to bed, "Are the clouds God?" I said to her, "No, God made the clouds." She thought a moment, and then said, "Was there any God before the coluds were made?" I said, "Yes, God had always lived." "I didn't know," said she. "Elizabeth said she didn't know." She then said she wanted to ask God to make her good. I let her get out and kneel down by her bed and offer her simple prayer, "My Father in Heaven wilt thou please to make me a good little girl." When she got back into her bed, I asked her if she was happy now, "Yes," she said, "very happy," and bade me good night. A few days after this I gave her the *Life of Rev. John Peak*, in which she found a portrait of this aged minister. "Was he a good man?" said she. I told her he was. Said she, "Can any people be as good as God?" "No," I said. "I thought," said she, "if they do'd as good as they could, they would be as good as God. I thought God didn't be any better than they, if they do'd as good as they could."

Caroline's affection for Laura seemed to increase rather than diminish by time and absence. She viewed her as a happy spirit in Heaven, and asked me one day if Jesus had little Laura in his arms, carrying her about. "What a dear little sister she was," she would frequently say. "I love her now she's in Heaven, I love her if she is in Heaven." At one time she said, "I love her soul and her body too." At another time, "I love her now she's in Heaven better than I did, because she's happier." Once when telling how lovely Laura was, she asked if Laura was not dearer to me than any one else. I said she was dear, but that I did not know that I loved Laura any better than I did her. "O," said she, "I think she was very dear, dearer than anybody else," and then after a moment's pause, as if correcting herself, "but God."

I think it was about this time, that is, soon after Laura's death, while her feelings and thoughts seemed so naturally to turn heaven-ward, that I began to take her regularly into a room with me before she retired, for prayer. At first I prayed with and for her, and occasionally she would ask me to let her pray after I had finished. I endeavored to keep this exercise as simple, and at the same time as pleasant to her, as possible. And it seemed to have a good effect. She would frequently say, after I had asked of the Lord a blessing upon the little one who had been spared to us, and that she might be a good girl, "I want to be a good girl all days." Gradually, and of her own accord, she took upon herself the regular performance of this duty. I always, unless prevented by ill health or some other cause, have attended her in her retirement, and have been at the same time particularly interested with her manner in prayer and also the effect of it upon herself. She generally seemed more affectionate, especially towards me, and usually on rising from her knees would kiss me and say, "What a dear Mother you are," or some similar expression of love. These things encouraged me to persevere, and though to this day I am not perfectly decided as to what is the best course to pursue in the religious education of a child, yet as I wished earnestly to train her up for Heaven, I have been unwilling to omit anything that *seemed* to be duty. I have endeavored to weigh the subject, and from all the light I can gather, have thought it the safest course to accustom a child to be in the *habit* of daily prayer.

July 22, 1841

It is summer again and we miss little Laura very, very much. I often think how happy Caroline would be, could she have her dear little sister to run in the fields with her. We have the music of the birds as sweet as we had last summer, but the sweet music of Laura's voice we hear no more. How consoling the thought, it is tuned to the high praises of God, and that if we are His children we shall meet her again where all is bright and happy.

Caroline enjoys pretty good health this summer but I think her nerves are in a more excitable state than they have been before for a year. She sleeps till quite late in the morning, and when she wakes, seems irritable until after she has had her breakfast. Any little thing troubles her at this time. But after breakfast she is generally happy through the day. She plays outdoors most of the day in good weather, and enjoys it very much. Two or three weeks since, she commenced going to Infant Sabbath School. She enjoys this very much, and is very happy in getting her little lessons ready. I have taken very little pains to teach Caroline to read, thinking healthy exercise better for her than study. She has learned almost wholly of her own accord, the alphabet, and the figures, and reads and spells in words of two letters, counts and recites the multiplication table through the first line, for amusement. She has a very retentive memory, and learns very easily. I was once reading to her the eighteenth chapter of Luke, and she was very much surprized and grieved with what is said about the treatment our Saviour was about to receive when he should be delivered up to the Gentiles, and should be mocked and spitted on. "What did they for? What did they for?" was all she could say for some time, as tears almost choked her utterance. After this she frequently desired

me to read, to hear "about those people that spit on our Saviour."
Soon she could repeat almost the whole of the chapter, giving the
emphasis correctly. She has learned to sew very neatly, all of her own
accord, and has already made herself quite useful in this way. She is
very fond of hemming, and besides hemming numerous little pieces
without name or use, has hemmed a set of sheets and pillow cases for
her little bedstead, and almost a whole piece of diaper for me. She is
now four-and-one-half years old.

August 18, 1841

About one-half past seven in the morning we were blessed in
the birth of a little son. He seemed from the first entirely different
from our other children. He weighed eight-and-one-half pounds,
seemed very strong and healthy, and withal so hungry that he made
repeated attempts to nurse within the first twenty-four hours.
Caroline had occasion again to rejoice, and her affection for him
has continued to increase daily. We named him Edward Buffum,
after his uncle. He is seven months old today, the eighteenth of
March, and until within about a month has enjoyed almost uninter-
rupted health. When he was three months old I believe he weighed
about fourteen pounds, as much as Caroline did at a year. His arms
at five months were larger than Caroline's at the same time, and she
was five years old. He now wears a pair of shoes that Laura wore
when she was seventeen months old, and they are so small that he
will soon outgrow them.

But notwithstanding his general health he has within the last
month been very near death. He took cold and seemed threatened with croup. He continued so for about two weeks, when he
began to be feverish, and we thought was threatened with lung
fever. We gave him castor oil and emetics, and hoped he would be
better, but on Thursday afternoon he began to cough and choke
and during the afternoon we had very little hope of his life. The
doctor providentially came in to see him just as this severe turn of
croup came on, and staid with him all the afternoon. He gave him
ipecac, and when that was not sufficiently powerful, antimony,
and kept him under the influence of emetics all the afternoon. He
spoke as if he thought it a very doubtful case, and even intimated

that he thought he would not live till night. And indeed he scarcely looked like a living child. His expressive blue eyes were sunk deep in their sockets and we thought his appearance could not change much by the touch of death. He was somewhat relieved before night, though he was very feverish, and we hardly expected he would live till the next morning, expecting in the course of the night a return of his distress in breathing. But he grew some better before morning, so that I retired about two o'clock, and left him in the care of an excellent, experienced woman. By Saturday he was decidedly better, and on Sabbath morning began to smile a little. After that he recovered very fast, and seems now to be very well, except that he is worrysome on account of his teething. He has two under teeth, just cut through, and two more upper ones, nearly through. He is very pleasant and playful, and seems to have a very healthy constitution and a happy disposition. He is very fond of strangers, and will go to any one who offers to take him, and will sometimes even seem to seek an acquaintance with them by holding out his hands to them, as if asking them to take him. In this respect he is very different from our other children. He does not creep yet but I think if it were warm enough for him to be down on the floor, he would soon learn.

August 6, 1842

A sad task devolves upon me now, that of recording the death of dear little Caroline, and her beloved brother, Edward. Little did I anticipate in making the last record of them that the next would be after their departure to the land of spirits. It is so, and we are left childless. Everything around us seems changed. Earth with its joyous birds and flowers has lost half its attractions, since one who loved so much the beauties of nature, is laid in the silent grave. Our walls do not now echo to the glad laugh and the free bound of those sweet little ones who were once the inmates of our happy dwelling. But if Earth is losing, I trust Heaven is increasing its attractions. We feel that, though taken from us, our children still live, and that in a peculiar and most endearing relation, they are united to us, and we may yet call them ours. We hope they are redeemed, and their robes made white by the precious blood of Christ, and that we shall one day stand before the throne with the children God has given us.

But I must go back and speak of things that were. In one of my last records of Caroline I mentioned her habit of daily prayer. I generally attended her in this exercise, but during the early part of the past winter she would sometimes prefer to go alone, especially if she had done anything wrong, for which she wished to ask the forgiveness of her heavenly Father. When with me she would thank the Lord for giving her a little brother, and pray that when he grew up he might be a good man. About this time Elizabeth Yerrinton, who lives with us, was, as we hoped, converted and joined the church. After this event Caroline almost invariably prayed that she might become a Christian, and made the same request for others, not forgetting the benighted heathen and the down-trodden slave. Her feelings had always been very much interested in the cause of temperance. She pitied the children of drunkards, and seemed thankful she had temperate parents. These feelings were chiefly elicited by pictures of scenes of intemperance, with its awful results, in the *Temperance Almanac,* and Dr. Jewett's *Youth's Temperance Lecturer.* One Sabbath day I retired with her, and she asked that all those who make or drink, I do not recollect which, rum, brandy, gin, wine, alcohol, whiskey and arrack, might give it up and become good sober men. She also prayed for Mr. Jennings, who was here on an exchange with her father, that the Lord would carry him safely home and that his little children might be glad to see him.

During the winter she gradually discontinued the practice of prayer, but always seemed willing to go with me, and generally would kneel quietly by my side while I endeavored to commend her to God. It was very painful to me to have her relinquish the habit of praying for herself, and I would sometimes ask her, when we went to my room, if she would not like to, although I never urged her to do it. She would say, "No, I don't think I'm prepared." It seemed as if in some measure the eyes of her understanding were opened to behold the holiness and extent of the moral law of God, and a sense of her own unworthiness led her to shrink from presenting herself in His presence.

I would sometimes ask her if she hoped she was a Christian. She would say, "I've no reason to think I am." She seemed in some measure to dread any moral or religious instruction, and manifested some little uneasiness under the application of truth. At the same time she would always gladly listen to any portion of Scripture, and seemed as much interested in the perceptive and doctrinal, as in the historical parts of the Bible. Sometimes she would ask questions which have puzzled older heads than hers. Questions which children at five years seldom think of asking. It was always her desire to understand the meaning of every word she heard used, and of every idea. Sometimes, I would say, "I don't think you can understand, I don't know as I can explain it to you." "Well, explain it as well as you can," she would say. And in this way she got an understanding of things that I should not have thought her old enough to be instructed in. She one day said to me, "Mother, you said that our Saviour was God, and the Son of God too. But no! that can't be, it is not so." I told her she must not say so, it was a mystery. I could not understand it, and there were a great many things which I could not understand, but we must believe that it was so, because the Bible says so. She said nothing more against it, but seemed to receive it by faith, and implicit confidence in my word.

At one time I told her that we supposed the stars were worlds somewhat like ours, and were inhabited. I should have said the planets, and that the fixed stars are supposed to be suns. A few days after she said to me, "Mother, you told me the other day that the stars were supposed to be worlds like this world, and that people live there. But no!", said she very emphatically, "it can't be. It may be for their souls, but not for their bodies, because they're so small." I told her they were not small, but only appeared so on account of their great distance from us. To illustrate this principle I told her that when I was a little girl there were some yellow balls on the spire of the academy at Smithfield where I went to school, and I thought they were small, about the size of an apple. But at one time there came a very high wind, and blew them down to the ground. As I was passing to school the next day I saw them lying by the roadside, and was very much astonished to find them so large—about as large as my head. I could hardly believe at first that they were the same. She seemed perfectly satisfied with this illustration, and made no further objection to it.

A short time after that, perhaps a week, she called me to look out the door and see some very large icicles pendant from the roof of the wood house. As I stood in the door way I reached up my hand to one of the largest and pulled it off without breaking it. As soon as I showed it to her she exclaimed, "O! I didn't know it was so long." Said I, "It is like—," "Like the stars," said she. I perceived she had not forgotten the lesson about the effects of distance on the apparent magnitude of things.

It was very interesting to teach her, because she received ideas so readily, and although we did not attempt to give her regular school learning, and never sent her to school except during one summer to Sabbath school, yet she was always learning. If we read anything she would listen with too intense an interest and inquire the meaning of every word she did not understand. So that she used language, in many instances, far above her years. For example, one day she was rolling a block to me across the room. After rolling it a few times, she changed her position, which brought her basket of playthings between her and me. She was going to roll the block, but seeing the basket, started, and took hold of it, saying, "O! here's an obstacle in the way."

She was very apt in learning anything and had a very retentive memory. She was much interested in the study of arithmetic, though we never taught it to her except for amusement. She would answer the questions in *Smith's Mental Arithmetic* sooner than a child of ten who was with us, and had been studying it all summer at school. She loved to count, and one day said she was going to count a thousand. I did not think she would have patience to go through with it, and should have been glad to have her desist from such a protracted effort of the mind. But she persevered until she had accomplished it, which she did, I think, in the course of an hour, with a very little help from me.

She learned to spell words of one syllable and to read a little. One little book of Edward's containing Scripture scenes she was fond of hearing read, and would sometimes read in it herself. But she learned a great deal that she never read. She knew the Commandments, the Lord's Prayer, several Psalms and a number of little hymns. She studied also the book of nature. Every flower, every bird, every insect and even every leaf and spire of grass was a page in which she could read the wonderful works of that forming hand which she recognized in everything around her. One day I called her to look at a dragonfly which I saw on the ground. She came, and glanced at it a moment, and then ran to get her primer in which she recollected there was a picture of that insect, and compared it with the real one. She one day came to me after having been out in the yard, and told me she saw some little ants building their nests. And then coming up close to me she said in a low subdued tone, "And, Mother when I saw them it made me think of, 'Go to the ant, thou sluggard.'" She had great reverence for the name of God and the word of God.

She was also a very affectionate and grateful child. She was ready to love everybody, even if they did not manifest any particular regard for her. But if she received attention of kindness from any one she did not soon forget it. And her expressions of gratitude and affection seemed to come warm from the heart. "O! thank you, thank you, dear Mother," she would sometimes say on getting into bed, especially after I had made it up clean, "thank you for making me such a nice bed."

Caroline was very discriminating. I one day said to little Eddie as he sat on the floor, "You are a good little boy." "O! no, Mother," said she, "he isn't good, for he doesn't know the difference between good and bad." "Well," said I, "he's a pleasant boy. You think there's no merit in it?" "No," said she.

She was very fond of playing "sell," in imitation of the peddlers who frequented the houses in the country, and would often load her little wagon with such commodities as she could gather from the house and yard, and draw it round, stopping occasionally at the door to ask if we would like to buy something. In return for the articles we purchased, we gave her little bits of wood or paper which we called money, and she never wished to put us to any trouble about it. If we were too busy to attend to it, she would lay down the article we bought and go to find something which she would call money. One day she took some squashes from the barn and put them in her wagon, and offered them for sale to her father. He asked the price, and she told him two cents apiece. He took one, and instead of paying her in the usual way, took two cents from his pocket and gave them to her. She looked at them with astonishment exclaiming, "Why, Father! You've given me real money and the squashes were yours before." She seemed almost unwilling to keep them, until her Father assured her he intended she should, and then she came and related the whole to me, expressing great surprise that her father should buy what was his own, and pay real money for it.

This incident leads me to speak more particularly of Caroline's honesty and strict regard for truth. She never would take the smallest thing that did not belong to her without leave, not even a lump of salt. And ever seemed to fear we should give her things sometimes which she ought not to have. "Mother," she would sometimes say, "may I have an apple? I've had one today." Or, "May I have a doughnut? I've had two today." Or, if I gave her either of the above named articles, of which she was very fond, she would frequently say, "Father gave me one this morning" or, "I've had one today." I do not recollect that she ever tried to deceive me, and if she had done wrong I always felt that I could trust her word to tell me all about it. She loved the truth, and believed everything that was said to her, and was very much grieved if any one spoke an untruth. One day I took her up in my lap to read to her from her little hymn book. There was one little story of a girl who told a falsehood, which I had purposely avoided reading to her, lest it should distress her. But at this time she pointed to that and asked me to read it. I thought, as she was now older than when she first had the book, I would read it, but I had not gone more than half through with it before she began to cry, saying, "O, what did she for, what did she for?" And I was obliged to use all the kindly efforts in my power to soothe her agonized feelings.

Caroline was generally obedient and easily governed, but there seemed to be a nervous impetuosity in her nature that sometimes led her into disobedience. For example, if she was jumping over a cricket and I said, "Caroline, don't jump over it again," she would in an instant be over. The impulse seemed to have been given and her quick and active temperament nerved for the effort, and the prohibition was unheeded. But she was always sorry, and I made allowance for her peculiar temperament, which to a stranger might appear like indulgence. We never but once, except in the first instance, were obliged to correct her for refusing to do what was required of her. In all other cases it was for this impulsive kind of disobedience. We wished to train her to a habit of implicit compliance with our directions, and on this account we frequently had occasion to correct her in such a way as we thought would best promote this object.

One day I was sitting in the parlor with the dear babe in my arms and Caroline was playing in the sitting room adjoining. I perceived she had taken the shovel and was drawing the ashes out of the fireplace upon the hearth. I spoke to her and told her to come to me. But being very busy she continued a few minutes at work with the shovel. I rose and went towards her, and she seeing me, started at the same time to come to me. I felt afraid that I had been too lenient with her in former instances of disobedience, and thought I must now do something that would make an abiding impression upon her mind. I took her into another room and expressed to her my regret on account of her disobedience, and told her that I would have to whip her now as she had disobeyed in the same way several times and I feared she would again. At the same time I endeavored to show her how wrong it was for her not to come when I first spoke to her. She seemed very penitent, and as she always dreaded that mode of punishment very much, more I think than any other child I ever saw, she entreated me not to inflict it, saying she would try to remember and obey *immediately* in the future. I considered her request and told her I would excuse her if she thought she should remember. As she never liked to have any one see her when she had been crying, I told her she might stay in that room until she had dried her tears so that she could look pleasant and then she might come out.

She got up into a chair by the window and I left her. After waiting some time, expecting she would come, and hearing nothing from her, I went to the room to inquire the cause of her staying so long. As I opened the door she came toward me with a sweet subdued look and taking my hand said in a low voice, "Mother, I think you better whip me. I am afraid I shan't remember." I cannot describe the feelings of that moment. To see that delicate little creature, whose dread of physical suffering, and especially of this kind of suffering, was so great that her language when she had transgressed was frequently, "O, don't have to whip me," or, "O, don't have to whip me hard!" to see her requesting me to do it was a trial to my feelings such as I had never anticipated, and was not prepared for. I told her I hoped she would remember, I did not love to punish her unless it was necessary. "O no!" said she sorrowfully, "I think you better whip me, I'm afraid I shan't remember." What could a mother do? I stooped towards her reluctantly to administer the correction she craved. At that moment the God of Abraham bade me stay my hand. "Would it not do as well," said I, "to ask God to help you remember?" "O yes! better," said she, and she knelt by my side, while I endeavored to commend her to the watchful care of Israel's gentle Shepherd. I do not recollect that she ever afterward disobeyed me in this way.

One instance, however, of disobedience of a different kind is most painful to remember. One in which she refused to do what was required of her. The circumstances were these. Polly Burr was spending a few days with us, and one morning when she first came into the sitting room, she, as usual, bade Caroline good morning. It was in the spring, and Caroline, as I said before, was feeble, and sometimes irritable in the morning. She loved Polly very much, but at this time did not return her morning salutation. I said to her, "Say good morning, Polly," not thinking but that she would readily comply. But she did not. I spoke again, when she said, "No," very decidedly. I told her if she did not say so I must put her into the bedroom, and let her stay there till she would. She still refused, and I took her into the bedroom, and after talking to her a little time, left her.

Presently I went to her again, but she refused to obey, and I thought it my duty to chastise her, which I did, but without any good effect, repeatedly. She did not seem angry, but on the contrary, very affectionate, would put her arms around my neck, and kiss me, and say, "Why don't I do it, Mother?" But there seemed to be a fixed determination not to do it. She did not cry excessively, but I never saw more of mental agony and internal conflict depicted on a countenance than hers had at that time. Once or twice she said, "O, it will kill me!" Not meaning the chastisement but the excitement of her feelings. I was distressed. I knew not what course to take. I thought of the famous story of Dr. Weyland's child, and feared she might hold out as long as he did. But she was so frail, I feared she would sink under such protracted resistance. Our breakfast was ready and all the family were waiting, but I felt that it was of the first importance that she should be brought to yield.

Her father was in the study, and overhearing, called me to tell me that I must not yield to her, as he feared my feelings would lead

me to, after having repeated the correction so many times, and continued it so long. I told him how decided she appeared, and he
came down and went into the room where she was with me. He
talked, and then prayed with her, and then I asked her if she would
obey. "No! I shan't!" said she. Words that I do not know that she
ever used on any other occasion. We were pained to the heart. It
seemed as if the enemy had her completely in his power, and was
trying to effect her ruin. As a last resort her father said he would go
out and procure a stick to whip her with; this we had never used, as
she had always yielded without any trouble. And if we ever were
obliged to inflict punishment it was not to make her do what we
wished her to, but for something she had done which she ought not
to do. Her father left the room on his painful errand, and she knew
that a more dreaded punishment than she had ever suffered awaited
his return. She sprang to me saying earnestly, "I will, I will." I
immediately gently led her out, almost trembling lest she should
shrink from it when put to the test. But she made an effort and as
soon as she got where Polly was said, "Good morning, Polly," and
I led her back, and when her father returned we were glad no further correction was necessary. I wiped away her tears and as breakfast had been waiting an hour or more we all sat down to the table.
Caroline seemed unusually mild and lovely, a sweet submissive spirit
seemed to influence all her conduct, and in the afternoon she said
to me, "I was very happy this morning at breakfast."

This was to us one of the most painful events of her life. It
showed us the depraved state of the unrenewed heart, even of a
gentle, lovely, and generally obedient child. I trust we were led by it
to pray more earnestly for the renewing influences of the Spirit of
God. Never before this had we felt so much the need of it. And we
cherish the hope that those prayers offered in weakness, though I
believe in sincerity, were heard for her before the throne of grace.
Though she never gave us, during health, any reason to hope that
her heart had been renewed, yet such gentleness and patience were
manifested during her last sickness, and such comfort and hope
vouchsafed to us when she was taken from us, that we rest in the
belief that, "The blood of Jesus Christ which cleanseth from all
sin," was applied to her soul. And we hope one day to meet all our
little ones among the redeemed in Heaven.

Caroline had a generous self-sacrificing disposition. She was always glad to share what she had with others. If anything nice was given her she always wanted to divide it. She thought Father should have the largest piece, Mother next, then Elizabeth, and herself the smallest. She would sometimes go upstairs with me into the storeroom and say, "Mother, may I have a walnut?" or, "May I have a cranberry?" And when I told her she might, would say, "May I have one for Elizabeth?" If she heard a story she would immediately run and communicate it to Elizabeth that she might be a sharer in her enjoyment. Sometimes she would start before it was finished, lest she should forget it. She loved to contribute to the various benevolent objects of the day, and one day when the famous Negro, Frederick Douglass, had been lecturing in our Meeting House, she got him to come home with us after Meeting that she might give him a piece of money for the cause of the poor slave. She kept her money in a little box, and one day when she had been looking at it she asked me how much there was of it. I told her there was more than a dollar. "O," said she, "how many Bibles it would buy for the poor heathen." Instead of thinking how she could spend it for her own gratification, she thought of those who were perishing for lack of knowledge. And the little fund together with that which belonged to her dear brother, amounting in all to two dollars and fifty-five cents, has been since their departure, sacredly devoted to that object.

Caroline was very affectionate and forgiving. She never seemed to manifest any resentment when corrected for her faults, but seemed to feel that it was necessary for us to do it, and after such correction, which we seldom had to administer, would seem even more affectionate than usual, clasping her arms around our necks and expressing her love for us. But if she was injured, she felt it keenly for the moment. Once when her Father was shaving, she came too near, and hit him, and he took hold of her arm rather severely, which he afterward regretted. "Father," said she, "you shouldn't take hold of me so." But in a few moments she was cheerful as before.

Evil and malicious passions seemed to have no abiding place in her breast. If they were ever suffered to enter, it was only for a few moments. It was not their home. That breast was the home of much that was lovely and good. I think she came as near fulfilling the great command "Love thy neighbor as thyself," as any one I have ever seen. Her heart seemed like a reservoir of love, ready to flow out whenever there was an object for it to fasten upon. It was not that fastidious kind of love that will not be pleased with an object unless it is exactly suited to one's own taste. She loved those very unlike herself, even if they did not manifest any particular affection for her. If she was treated unkindly, it seemed to make no difference. She seldom spoke of it, but seemed to love to dwell on the favors she received. She loved to enumerate the friends and relatives she had, and would sometimes mention particularly all her little cousins by name, and then add, "And Franky, he's my little friend." This little son of Dr. Stanley's was indeed a dear friend and playmate, and a sincere mourner after her death. Once she got me to write the names of her cousins in a book, so that she could see them, and Frank's name was added to the list.

She possessed a very retentive memory, and uncommon ingenuity to execute what she saw others do. She learned to sew, and to braid, for her own amusement, and if she had lived, would doubtless have made herself useful as far as her health would admit. She was very fond of cutting pictures, and drawing on a slate. One Sabbath day I showed her a picture of Mrs. Judson's grave under the Hopia tree. Two or three days after, she had her slate and pencil, and being left alone in the sitting room a few minutes, drew a very correct picture of it. When I came into the room she showed it to me, and I was astonished at the accuracy with which it was drawn, merely from memory. When she looked at anything she examined it very attentively. She would take a geography, or any other book with pictures, and sit entirely engrossed with it for half an hour or more. She seemed to *read* them, and they conveyed distinct ideas to her mind.

Many a time has she wept bitterly over the *Temperance Lecturer* and *American Anti-Slavery Almanac*, merely from having of her own accord studied the pictures, till her soul seemed to be filled with their meaning. We put them out of her reach when we found how they affected her. But she had a heart "to feel for others' woe," and if she had lived would doubtless have suffered much from sympathy.

In April of 1842, we went to Bridgewater to attend the wedding of Lucy Lovell, the daughter of Shubael S. Lovell, my husband's brother, who was to be married to John Hancock Brown of Franklin Furnace, New Jersey. Little Eddie was then about eight months old, Caroline five years. She enjoyed the visit very much, and Eddie was the affection of all who became acquainted with him. He seemed more shy of strangers than when at home, but on the whole was very pleasant and lovely. Caroline was gentle and good. When we came home it was very cold and she suffered a good deal in consequence, so that we were obliged to stop several times and let her warm her feet. In riding she usually stood nearly all the time, so that she became fatigued sooner, and suffered more with the cold. She wanted to notice every object as we passed, and would sometimes want to get out, and go to examine a house if there was anything unusual in the construction of it. She noticed also the trees and flowers as we passed, and would frequently solicit her father to get out and pick such flowers as pleased her, which he sometimes did.

Soon after we returned home from Bridgewater we visited sister Elizabeth Chace at Valley Falls. Here the children had a very pleasant time. Caroline and John Gould Chace had many fine plays together, although Johnny was not very well, so that we could not go out of the house. Little Oliver Chace too was sick, and Sister supposed they were both coming down with the measles. In about two weeks after we returned home, Caroline and Edward were both taken sick, and confined to the chamber about a week. I supposed that Edward had the measles and something of croup. He was stuffed a good deal every night, and a slight eruption was visible, but we could not be sure, as he was not much sick, and we did not feel certain that he had been exposed to the measles. Caroline was confined to the bed several days, and seemed to have some fever but no eruption. She wasted very much, and was never so strong afterward. After she had nearly recovered, Mrs. Olivia Stanley called to see me, and brought Frank with her, but left him out in the barn where Mr. Lovell then was, fearing that he might take the measles of Edward. But Caroline stood at the window and saw him, and was very anxious to have him come in. Mrs. Stanley finally consented to run the risk of exposing him to the measles and he came in, and came up to see her. In a few days more they were both pretty well and I took them downstairs.

Spring had now come and opened the buds and brought up the tender shoots, and Caroline loved to watch their growth. Her Father gave her and Elizabeth each a little plot of ground in the garden, and I assisted them in planting the seeds. Caroline was very happy in putting the seeds into the ground, or in tripping across the field to see and gather the wild flowers, or in pulling up weeds for the pig. When the hay was cut she enjoyed it very much, for her father allowed her to help gather it up, and it was pleasant to see her little feet tripping so merrily across the field, and to hear her sweet voice saying, "The flowers are blooming in my path to school." Edward too, could now ride out in his little wagon, and this Caroline enjoyed as much as he did, for she loved to see him happy. Her Aunt Sarah Buffum Borden had been here in the winter and had taught Caroline something of botany, and now she was very busy in applying her little store of knowledge. As soon as the lilacs bloomed she wanted me to help her analyse the flowers, and pressed quite a number of flowers to carry to Aunt Sarah and Uncle Nathaniel when we should go to Fall River in the summer, as we expected to.

During the illness of the children, which I have mentioned, we received a letter from Brother Lorenzo Lovell, saying that he intended to visit us, and we were now expecting him soon, with his wife and little Richard, who was near Caroline's age. Caroline looked forward to the visit with unusual interest.

They arrived in the evening of the last Wednesday of May, just as Caroline had gone up to go to bed. She heard the carriage as they came up in the yard, and was very anxious to know if cousin Richard had come. I came down and found him here and they all went up to see her. She embraced little cousin with apparent affection although they had never met before since they were old enough to recognize each other. They had many pleasant plays the three following days. On Saturday we went over to the burying ground to visit Laura's grave. The children went with us. Caroline seemed very happy. She picked quite a number of wild flowers that grew around the graves and brought them home to press.

On the next morning about three o'clock she awoke and seemed restless and threw off the bedclothes. Her Father spoke to her and told her not to throw them off. She did not complain but continued restless, and I got up and lighted a lamp. In a few minutes she vomited. I began to think she was coming down with the measles, and supposed she had taken them of Frank Stanley when he was here, the day before he was sick with them. She continued to vomit occasionally for the space of three or four hours, suffering extremely from nausea when not vomiting. As soon as it was light I discovered an eruption coming out on her face and hands. About this time I think her mind began to wander.

About seven o'clock we brought her down and put her into the bed in the little bedroom adjoining the sitting room. Her mind seemed to wander considerably during the day, and she suffered a great deal from nausea, but did not vomit any more after about seven o'clock. Before noon the eruption was out all over her body, and assumed a dark reddish appearance. She talked a good deal about her play, and spoke frequently of cousin Richard. She seemed very mild and patient. I watched by her bed during the day with painful anxiety. Though I then supposed she had the measles, and our physician had pronounced it a case of measles, yet I felt alarmed. She was so frail I feared she would not endure even an attack of the measles. If I had known it was that awful scourge, scarlet fever, I should have had still less hope for her. The doctor told us to keep her very quiet and not give her much medicine at present.

Sabbath night her father took care of her and I slept upstairs with the babe.

Monday morning Brother Lorenzo and his wife and little Richard left for Providence. Mr. Lovell intended to go with them as far as Providence, and then go from there to Fall River, to see once more his dear dying brother, Leander. But Caroline seemed so sick that he concluded not to go. She continued about the same Monday as the day before. At any rate we thought she grew no worse, and hoped she was a little better. Monday night Mrs. Elijah Bates watched with her. She called, "Mother," in the night so loud that I came down to her, and spoke to her, and she grew more quiet. I would gladly have staid with her if I had not had a nursing babe upstairs. In the morning when her father came down and went into the bedroom she said to him, "Father, I want you to stay with me all the time." Her father felt very anxious to see his brother once more, and thought if he did not go immediately he should not see him alive, and as Caroline seemed no worse, but rather more comfortable, and as we did not apprehend any immediate danger in her case, we concluded it was best for him to go. He left home Tuesday, expecting to stay one day with his brother, and return Thursday, and probably reach home Thursday evening.

After he left Caroline grew worse. Mrs. Bates Thayer, who staid with me to help take charge of her, had her in her arms about eleven o'clock while I tried to comb and braid her hair to make her more comfortable. I stood behind so that she did not see me. She called for Mother. I stepped round in front of her and said, "Here I am." "Where?" said she. "I don't see you." I told her I was close by her. "No," said she, "that isn't Mother, you don't wear a cap." I thought then that she had lost her sight, and felt more alarmed than I had been before. But she soon recovered it again. From this time, however, she seemed to grow worse. Her breathing was deep and quick, and her fever was high. Her mind seemed at times very dull, at other times irregular. The doctor came in about noon, and we moved her into the parlor, that she might have more air. She did not notice the change of rooms at all, and I do not think ever realized that we moved her. She slept a good deal, and when she waked would seem lost for a few moments.

It was my privilege to sit by her bed most of the time, so that when she woke she almost invariably found me there. She would put both her hands upon my face gently, and say in an affectionate voice, "Who is this—Mother?" And when I assured her it was, she would say, "O, I didn't know." In the forenoon of this day I gave her some medicine, and she took it very well. I said to her, "You are a dear little girl, you do just as Mother wants you to." She seemed pleased, and looked up very affectionately at me and said, "I 'most want to hug you." I put my neck down for her to put her arms round it, but she was so weak that she could not do it alone. I put them round my neck and asked her to kiss me. Her lips were very sore, and she tried to kiss me but could not. "I would if I could," said she, "I would if I could, but I can't."

In the evening of Tuesday she seemed to grow worse. She called for water a great many times, and when it was brought she would put it from her mouth. She said she wanted a quart of water, and asked the doctor to get a fresh pail full. Then she would say, "Where shall we put this pail of water?" We concluded it was best to send for her father the next morning. Nancy Scott watched with her that night, and I took the babe downstairs and slept in the bedroom. I sat up till about eleven and then left her with Nancy, who I knew would watch her very attentively. Before I lay down I mentioned that she generally called "Mother," when she first woke, and told Nancy if she said, "Mother," to ask her what she wanted instead of telling her I was not there. Soon after I had gone to sleep she woke, and as usual spoke to me, supposing I was there. Nancy went to her and asked what she wished. Said she, "Mother, I want to kiss you." Nancy put her face down and she kissed very affectionately till Nancy thought it would fatigue her and left her. But she was not satisfied. She called again, "Mother, I want to kiss you again." After repeating this token of love which I should have prized so highly, she sank into sleep. She never was able to kiss me during her whole sickness.

Early Wednesday morning Mr. Cushman started for Fall River to hasten her father's return. We felt that her life must be short, and knew that it would be doubly afflictive to him if she was taken from us during his absence. On Wednesday in the afternoon Brother Lorenzo came from Providence with Dr. Waterman, hoping that his advice might be beneficial. But our physician had gone to another part of the town and he could not consult with him, and of course could do nothing. He thought it was a very severe case of measles. He advised bathing with weak lye and a poultice of slippery elm, both of which I adopted.

Caroline, although so very sick, knew her Uncle Lorenzo, and enquired if Richard had come. Frank Stanley came in to see her and she knew him and gave him her hand. She asked the doctor to let him stay, saying, "I think I should get well quicker." He told her Frank might come in again by and by. In the afternoon she said she wished the doctor would come in, "And Franky too," said she, "he's a little of a doctor."

Elizabeth Yerrinton came and stood by her bed, I think it was Wednesday, and she spoke and said, "I don't want Elizabeth to stand there, she looks like a new girl." "And Franky too," she said, "looks like a new boy." She loved them but the aspect of things was changing.

Wednesday evening she seemed very sick. Her breathing was very difficult, and we feared she would not live till morning. Mrs. Thomas watched. About one half past ten her father came. She seemed to take no particular notice of him. Towards midnight she seemed more comfortable and we rested a little.

Thursday, she seemed brighter, and remarkably pleasant and lovely. She seemed pleased with some flowers that Elizabeth brought for her, counted them and asked if one of them was cinque-foil. She requested that she might be taken up and expressed a particular desire that her father should take her. This he esteemed a great privilege. Early in the afternoon, being very much exhausted, I went upstairs to lie down a few minutes, leaving my place at her bedside to be occupied by her father. Tired as I was with watching and anxiety I slept much longer than I intended, perhaps two hours. Caroline woke and called for me. Her father not wishing to disturb me, soothed her, and diverted her attention to something else, and she presently fell asleep. But on waking she renewed the request for Mother. Her father again waited upon her, and turned her attention. Presently she spoke out in a very earnest manner, "Can't you find my dear Mother?" This was irresistible and I was called. She had nothing particular to say to me when I came down, but seemed to have forgotten all about it.

She noticed her little brother in the afternoon and said, "He looks very lovely." When she heard him cry once, she said, "I don't feel so bad as he does." She tasted of an orange that her grandmother sent, and seemed pleased with it. She also noticed people who came in to see her, and spoke frequently of Dr. Waterman, who prescribed the slippery elm poultice for her blister, which had relieved the irritation very much.

Miss Emily Green, who had sewed for me in the spring, and had spoken of dressing Caroline's doll, came in Thursday afternoon to see her. Caroline knew her and said to her, "You didn't come to dress my doll while I was well, Emily." Towards night Dr. Metcalf called with Dr. Stanley. They gave us no encouragement. By nine o'clock a stupor seemed to be coming over her, which told us too plainly that death was doing its work. In the morning she had spoken of riding out with her father when she got well. She seemed sensible that she was very sick, and once said to me, "A few days ago I was *very* well—and a few hours ago I was *pretty* well, and now I'm *very* sick." She spoke of her Uncle Leander and said she should like to see him once more before he died. I told her he was going to Heaven when he died, and then remarked to her, "You are very sick, and we do not know that you will ever get well, would you like to die too, and go to be with Uncle Leander, if it is the will of God?" She answered very promptly, "Yes," and then after a moment's pause said, "If I can go to the good world— I don't want to go to the wicked world." I have regretted since that I did not repeat to her the sweet words of our Saviour, "Suffer little children to come unto me, and forbid them not: for of such is the kingdom of God." But it did not occur to me then.

She seemed to be unconscious of our presence after nine o'clock, and as we had lost our sleep in a great measure every night for nearly a week, we concluded to lie down and get a little rest, leaving her in the care of Mrs. Bates Thayer, an excellent friend of ours, who promised to call us if any change occurred during the night. Her fever still was high and the physician had told us he thought she would continue with us till morning. About three o'clock her fever abated and her breathing and general appearance changed so much that Mrs. Thayer spoke to us.

We stood by her bed to see the lamp of life go out. She had said nothing during the night. Her pains seemed to have left her. Surely the bitterness of death was past. There was no struggle. Nothing to indicate that death was there, but the low faint breath and the pallid countenance. Her end was peaceful. I kneeled down by the bedside and placing my ear near her mouth listened to the low breathing of the "sweet dying child." About four o'clock the sound died away and as the sun rose clear and all nature seemed to be rejoicing, her spirit was borne away to Him who gave it. O, if there ever was a guiltless soul on earth, since our blessed Saviour's passion, it seems to me hers was one. We felt our hearts sink within us, and the feelings that had long been pent up there, now burst forth in an agony of grief. We looked out towards the east where the sun was rising, we looked at the flowers that bloomed around our door, we listened to the music of the birds, but all seemed changed. I felt then that the world could never be to me what it had been.

We went for Mrs. Ellery Thayer to dress her for the grave. I combed her hair and braided it, as I had so many times done, and tied the ends with a narrow white ribbon. I felt that it was a great privilege to do it once more for her. During the day, which was Friday, the third of June, I think we were divinely supported, and felt willing to give her back to God. One thing only troubled me, the uncertainty with regard to the state of her soul. I sought an answer of the Lord, but He doubtless, for wise reasons, withheld it. O, I thought if I could only be sure that she was happy, that her soul had been washed and made white in the blood of the Lamb, I could then be entirely reconciled to the bereavement.

These feelings continued three days. I could not fix my mind upon anything definite with regard to her. I wanted to think of her among the ransomed spirits that surround the throne, and my prayer was that the Lord would be pleased to give me some assurance of her state. It seems to me now almost like presumption, but I did not realize it then. I felt so anxious for her soul. I did not think she was lost, but I could not think of her anywhere in particular. Friday night my husband proposed getting some young ladies to watch in the house, as is customary. I told him I wished he would procure those who would feel love for Caroline from having been acquainted with her, and would be very careful. Two young ladies in whom we had the most confidence, expressed that they felt it to be a privilege to sit up, and we consigned the care of the precious remains to them for the night. On Saturday afternoon she was buried. The funeral services were conducted at our house. Brother James Boomer, from Wrentham, spoke words of comfort and consolation to us.

Many of the neighbors came in to weep with us. Brother and sister Samuel B. and Elizabeth Chace, with their children, and sister Lydia Buffum Read, came from Valley Falls. On Saturday afternoon June 4, 1842, just one week from the day on which she had visited the graveyard with us, we laid Caroline by the side of her dear sister Laura.

• • •

Would that I might end here this writing which in the very doing has caused the wound in my heart to bleed afresh.

But our suffering was to be still more keen.

At this time our dear little Edward was well, the perfect picture of health and happiness, not at all realizing his loss but rejoicing in the love of all who knew him.

On the Sabbath I left him with Elizabeth Yerrinton and attended Meeting twice. Sister Elizabeth Chace was here with her children, and as it was unusually warm and pleasant, I did not feel afraid to leave him. After Meeting, Elizabeth went and sat on the front stairs with him, and we could hear his merry voice as we were at the tea table, and it helped to comfort us and drive away our sorrow. On Thursday, the day before Caroline died, her father had said to her, "You are Father's dear little daughter. All the little daughter that Father has." "Yes," said she very sweetly, "but you have a little son." Thus she comforted him.

My husband was at this time exhausted with watching, and the labor of the Sabbath, having baptized several that day. And we feared he was going to be sick. I felt at that moment as if God was about to visit me with still greater afflictions. If my husband, and only remaining child should be taken, what should I do? I felt reproved for my anxiety about Caroline, and was enabled, as I trust, to yield not only her soul, but the precious lives of my husband and child to Him who is "too wise to err, too good to be unkind." And in that moment of darkness, light broke in upon my mind. In submission to His will, whatever it might be, I found peace. It seemed to me that I could give them all up, hard as it would be, without a murmuring word or thought. And from that moment I have felt no anxiety about Caroline. Much comfort have I had in thinking of her happy state. When her Uncle Leander P. Lovell heard of her death, he remarked, "She will make an active little saint." He followed her in a week to the world of spirits. I have often thought of her active mind, so desirous to understand all mysteries, expanding and maturing under the instruction of Him who spoke as never man spoke, and taught as One having authority.

But to return to the dear babe. Two days after Caroline was taken from us, Edward became ill. I cannot again bear to tell the story of suffering which came to this last of our children. Our despair was utter when the physicians told us that he was afflicted with scarlet fever, the disease which they now had decided had taken Caroline. Sister Elizabeth Chace's little boy, John Gould, who attended Caroline's funeral, had been seized with the same illness on his return home, and lived only about two days, suffering beyond description. He had died on Wednesday. A little girl in our own neighborhood also had died after a short sickness of forty-eight hours. We felt horribly hopeless and desperate.

Our friends were so kind. Dr. Stanley spent all of the time he could spare in our parsonage, and did everything humanly possible. Mrs. Bates Thayer and Mrs. Thompson took turns with us in sitting up. On Sunday, a week after Edward had been taken ill, Mr. Rockwood, one of our dear friends who was a retired minister living in Bellingham, preached instead of my husband, so he could be with us at Edward's bedside. Mrs. Andrew Bates and Mrs. Mary-Ann Thayer also watched several nights.

My babe's constitution was so strong that the struggle for life had lasted ten days. His suffering was more than we could bear. And when at a quarter before eight on Tuesday evening the fourteenth of June his little spirit took its flight, we felt it was a happy release enabling him to join his much loved sister in that world of joy and peace where sickness and death can never enter. I took the little body I had so often dressed from the arms of Mrs. Bates Thayer, and handed it to Mrs. Ellery Thayer, and requested her to dress it for the grave. She had dressed him on the first bright morning of his happy existence, and now was about to dress him for the silent grave as she had kindly performed the same mournful duty for his sisters. We received many tokens of kindness and affection from our friends in Bellingham which much endeared them to us. May the Lord reward them!

I have often thought how joyfully Caroline would welcome her sweet brother to the realms of bliss. On Thursday afternoon his funeral was attended at our house. Brother Rockwood addressed us from the words "And in the garden there was a sepulcher." His object was to show that sorrow is mingled with joy in this world. He also referred to a remark made by Brother Boomer at Caroline's funeral that, "affliction often treads upon the heel of affliction." He alluded to the death of our daughter only twelve days before this dear child was taken from us, and also to John Gould, sister Elizabeth Chace's son, that rosy boy whom he had seen here on the occasion of her funeral, but who was now with his cousin Caroline in another world.

We laid little Edward by the side of his sisters, and it is a dear spot to us. We love to wander there and to think of each one of them separately as they were when with us, and then lift our eyes in faith to Heaven and behold them there together in love, a sweet little trio.

We were much comforted after Edward's death by thinking of the past. His little life looked to us like a pleasant dream. We felt thankful that so joyous a being was lent us a few brief months to cheer and gladden our hearts. I think we were divinely supported, and trust we felt from the heart to give him back to God. True, we felt exceedingly lonely after all were gone, and we heard their merry voices no longer, and had not even the mournful satisfaction of administering to their wants by the bed of languishing, but we knew they were with One who could, out of His immeasurable fulness, supply all their wants and train them better than we could.

On Friday, the next day after Edward was buried, I took Caroline's playthings, gathering them together from all parts of the house, and put them away in order. I put away their clothing also. While I did this it occupied my mind, and I thought not of myself. I spent nearly the whole day in this way. Saturday morning when we rose all was still about the house, and all in order, the playthings had staid just where I put them the day before. I looked in vain for some token of childish play. The order and stillness of the house oppressed me. I sank under it. A languor came over my whole system, a prostration of all my energies.

June 1843

A year has passed away since our dear little ones were taken from us. Our hearts still bleed. And bleed afresh as the opening of spring has reminded us of the past, and the approaching summer seems to say to us that we shall have no little ones to share with us its delicious flowers and fruits. But though, as time rolls away, we feel our loss more instead of less than at first, yet we trust the same power that sustained us then, upholds us now, and enables us in submission to say, "Not our will, but Thine, O God, be done."

• 4 •

My Anti-Slavery Reminiscences

by Elizabeth Buffum Chace,

Written in 1891

To my beloved son and daughters, I dedicate this record of a portion of my life, in the remembrance of which, among many failures and shortcomings, I now, in the eighty-fifth year of my age, find the most entire satisfaction. And I hope that they and their children may gather therefrom some lessons of adherence to principle and devotion to duty, at whatever cost of worldly prosperity or advancement.

I am ashamed to say that my early Quaker ancestors in Newport, Rhode Island, were interested in the slave trade. As a matter of fact Newport was quite an active slave market and ships came into the wonderful harbor there direct from Africa and much of their human cargo was disposed of in that village and redistributed to other sections. The leading families engaged in shipping and trade in Newport considered the slave trade as part of their legitimate business. Early in the history of Newport and Rhode Island, however, our family, the

Goulds and the Coggeshalls, all Quakers, gave up this business and frowned on the continued dealing in humans. For many generations my family must have constituted a large portion of the Society of Friends there—the first date of the existence of said society, in its original *Book of Discipline*, being 1675.

As the spirit of early Quakerism came to realize the terrible iniquity of the slave trade the Yearly Meeting of the Friends in 1727 issued advices and remonstrances against it, the first recorded being as follows:

"It is the sense of this meeting that the importation of Negroes from their native country is not a commendable practice, and that practice is censured by this meeting."

In 1760 the Yearly Meeting issued another advice to Friends, "to keep their hands clear of this unrighteous gain of oppression," and yet without absolute prohibition. In 1773, "It is recommended to Friends, who have slaves in possession, to treat them with tenderness, impress God's fear in their minds, promote their attending places of religious worship, and give those who are young, at least, so much learning that they may be capable of reading." The same year they also advise that "the young, and also the aged and impotent, be set free." The last record in the *Book of Discipline* is dated 1780, and disposes of the matter thus: "Agreed, that no Friend import, or any ways purchase, dispose of, or hold mankind as slaves; but, that all those who have been held in a state of slavery be discharged therefrom; that all those be used well who are under Friends' care, and are not in circumstances, through nonage or incapacity, to minister to their own necessities; and that they give to those who are young, such an education as becomes Christians, and encourage others in a religious and virtuous life." Thus the New England Yearly Meeting, held in Newport, Rhode Island, abolished slavery among its members in the year 1780, while it was still legalized by the New England States.

My grandmother, Sarah Gould, was born near the year 1737, and her father, James Coggeshall, soon after her birth purchased a little African girl from a slave ship just come into port, to serve as nursemaid to the child. She remained a slave in the household until the Friends abolished slavery among themselves in 1780, when, becoming a free woman, she established herself as a cakemaker and confectioner in the town, and lived esteemed and respected to a very old age. In my very infancy, my mother, Rebecca Gould Buffum, used to tell to my sisters and me the story of this girl, Morier, who was stolen from her home and brought up a slave in our great-grandfather's house; and of the strength of her attachment to our grandmother, whom she nursed in infancy. My mother remembered, as a child, her frequent visits to the homestead, and the affectionate welcome which always greeted her there. But, in all this story, which made a strong impression on our minds, our gentle mother gave us no idea that she thought it was ever right to buy little girls and hold them as slaves, although it was done by her own grandfather; so that we never had any predilections in favor of slavery.

In my childhood, my father, Arnold Buffum, used to tell us how, as a little boy, he stood between the knees of an escaped slave, Pedro, and listened to his tales of the sufferings of the slaves, of their capture in Africa, the miseries of the slave-ship, and of his own adventures in the escape with his family; the fond Negro father ending by placing his hand on the curly head of his youngest child, and exclaiming, "And Pedro love Cuffie better than all his children, cause he be free born." And so my father became an Abolitionist in his childhood; and his detestation of the "sum of all villanies" grew with his growth and strengthened with his strength, and never weakened or wavered throughout his long life.

When the Colonization Society was formed, he gave in his adhesion to that, in the belief, shared by many other good men, that this was the way out of the terrible evil. When Benjamin Lundy came with his appeals for gradual abolition, he hoped for rescue by this means, but when William Lloyd Garrison raised the cry for "immediate and unconditional emancipation," my father's clear head, his tender heart, and his unshrinking conscience, embraced, without doubt or question, the principles of the Garrisonian anti-slavery movement. He became the first president of the New England Anti-Slavery Society, and lived and labored in and for the cause for the rest of his life, though obloquy and persecution pursued and assailed him therefore. Thus was I born and baptized into the anti-slavery spirit. Our family were all Abolitionists, my father and mother, my sisters Sarah, Lucy, Rebecca and Lydia, their husbands Nathaniel Borden, Nehemiah Lovell, Marcus Spring and Clement Read, my aunt Patience Buffum who married Pliny Earle, and their children, my cousins, Eliza and her husband William Hacker of Philadelphia, and Thomas, and his wife Mary Hussey Earle of Germantown, and Pliny, Jr. Many other cousins were warm heartedly for the cause but had less opportunity to actively assist.

Never, in our large household, do I recall one word short of condemnation of the vile system. In our minds there were no palliating circumstances. The slave-holders were man-stealers; and, as one of the earliest of the lecturers used constantly to declare, they must "quit stealing." When I married Samuel B. Chace, and I called his attention to the question, he soon accepted the anti-slavery principles, and remained faithful thereto during his life.

Up to the time of the issue of the first number of the *Liberator* in the year 1831, we had believed there should be devised some scheme for gradual emancipation, as did our father. Soon after that my father came to my home in Fall River, and brought us the new paper and told us of having met William Lloyd Garrison and of having heard his arguments. He told us of the forming of the New England Anti-Slavery Society and I remember asking him if he thought it would be quite safe to set the slaves free all at once. In a few words, he dispelled, once for all, that illusion from my mind; and from that hour we were all Garrisonians. I remember well how eager we were, in our revived anti-slavery zeal, to present the cause of the slave to everybody we met; not doubting that, when their attention was called to it, they would be ready, as we were, to demand his immediate emancipations. But, alas! their commercial relations, their political associations, and with many, their religious fellowship with the people of the South, so blinded the eyes, hardened the hearts and stifled the consciences of the North, that we found very few people who were ready to give any countenance or support to the new anti-slavery movement.

My father and mother were, by inheritance, by education and by conviction, members of the Society of Friends; and were devoted to its principles, its service and mode of worship; and their children, being also birthright members, had been taught great reverence and respect for its Ministers and Elders, as well as for all the doctrines and peculiar customs of the Society; the idea of infallibility, without using the word, was, at that time, strong in the family mind. So, from the Friends, surely, we expected sympathy and co-operation. But, as we met them, individually or in groups, and made our appeal for the slave, we were shocked to find out even they whose forefathers had abolished slavery among themselves, while it was still legalized by the State, and had inserted in their *Book of Discipline* the advice to be often read, "That Friends be careful to maintain our testimony faithfully against slavery," had become so demoralized, that they too, with rare exceptions, shut their eyes to the great iniquity. They objected to the strong, denunciatory language of the *Liberator*; they disapproved of Friends uniting with other people in public meetings or in philanthropic work; they did not think the slaves should be set free all at once, and they did not want their daughters to marry Negroes. I remember making an appeal to a Quaker cousin of mine, by asking him if he did not think the slaves should be freed, and his only reply was, "I shouldn't want to see a black man sitting on the sofa beside my daughter."

We went to our Yearly Meeting at Newport, and there slavery was the chief topic of conversation, at the hotel where many Friends were staying; so stirred were people everywhere, either for or against the system, by the new awakening. But almost everybody was against us. They denounced the *Liberator*; Garrison was an infidel; slavery could only be cut off gradually; the colored race must be colonized in Africa. Joseph Bowne, a distinguished preacher from New York, was heard to declare, that, if he could set all the slaves free within thirty years, by turning over his hand, he would not do it. In the meeting we were cautioned by our Ministers not to give way to excitement, but to keep in the quiet and wait for divine guidance; and not to unite with people outside of our religion in public undertakings. Those who had already made themselves obnoxious in these ways, were ignored in the appointment of committees; and some who stood on standing committees were dropped therefrom. There was a general treatment of such as were known to be Abolitionists, as suspicious persons—persons to be overlooked and avoided.

I had, from my childhood, been a devout believer in and defender of orthodox Quakerism. I had been overseer of the poor in Swanzey Monthly Meeting, its assistant clerk, and finally its clerk; and had, in various ways, "been made use of," as the phrase was in the Society. I wore the Quaker costume in its entirety, and had never said "you" to a single person in my life, or given the title of "Mr." or "Mrs." to anybody. I was constant in the attendance of our religious Meetings, and firmly believed in the efficacy of our simple, and as we called them, unceremonious modes of worship. But to be an Abolitionist put me down among the ostracized.

I remember, on one occasion, at the Yearly Meeting, when an epistle, prepared to be sent to a distant Yearly Meeting, was read by the clerk and presented for approval, which contained the usual formula of the declaration of our testimony against the enslavement of "Africans," I objected to this designation, as most of the slaves in this country, at that time, were natives of America. Another anti-slavery woman seconded my remonstrance, and finally the word was changed. We afterward learned, that a Friend present from Philadelphia, inquired, " *Who those young women*," were, and expressed her surprise that our protest was heeded, "as such a proposal coming from a person *in the body of the house*, would be entirely unnoticed in Philadelphia Yearly Meeting."

At that time, the prejudice against color, throughout New England, was even stronger than the pro-slavery spirit. On one occasion, my husband and I went to Boston, to attend the annual meeting of the New England Anti-Slavery Society. Accompanied by a gentleman we drove to Taunton from Fall River, there to take the railroad, which at that time furnished only one car for the journey. As we entered the car, Samuel Rodman, an anti-slavery leader from New Bedford, and a highly respectable, well-dressed colored man and his wife, from the same town, also took seats therein. The conductor came and ordered the colored people to leave the car. We all remonstrated, of course, but without avail. He called the superintendent, who peremptorily repeated the order. The colored couple got out quietly, and we did the same, but not so quietly, and retired to the waiting-room, leaving the car empty. The officials held a conference outside, and the conductor soon informed us that an extra car had been put on for the Negroes, and invited us to take the seats we had left. We held a little conference among ourselves, and then every one of us entered the car with the colored people. The superintendent was very angry, but he did not quite dare to order us out, so he assured us that our conduct would avail nothing, for no Negroes would ever be permitted to be mixed up with white people on that road. They were mixed up with us, however, on that day, and we found them intelligent, agreeable companions.

In some cases, persons who were opposed to slavery and were willing to work for its abolition, nevertheless strongly objected to any association with colored persons in their anti-slavery labors. We organized a Female Anti-Slavery Society in Fall River, about the year 1835.

I recently came across some old papers and in going through them I found a list of the original members of this Female Anti-Slavery Society, written in the hand of the secretary. I list them exactly as they appeared.

Laura Lovell	Phebe Buffington
Sarah P. Buffum	Caroline P. Alden
Sarah Talbot	Jane H. Glazier
Lucy T. Shaw	Elizabeth R. Harris
Ariadne B. Lovell	Eliza Ann P. Fish
Lucy Buffum	Lydia Buffum
Lydia B. Cathcart	Ann Wilbur
Martha B. Lovell	Sarah D. Harris
Irene B. Luther	Mary M. Shaw
Sarah A. Woods	Maryann Paine
Sarah B. Luther	Mary L. Olden
Elizabeth B. Chace	Sarah Arnold
Avis A. Reynolds	Phebe Hussey

Louisa Lincoln

Of the twenty-seven original members, four were my own family, my sisters Sarah, Lucy, Lydia, and myself, and two were sisters of the man Lucy later married, the Reverend Nehemiah Lovell, Laura Lovell and Martha Lovell; and a third, Ariadne B. Lovell, was the wife of Leander P. Lovell, a brother of Nehemiah Lovell.

In the village of Fall River were a few very respectable young colored women, who came to our meetings. One evening, soon after the Society was formed, my sister Lucy and I went to see these Negro women and invited them to join. This raised such a storm among some of the leading members, that for a time, it threatened the dissolution of the Society. They said they had no objection to the women attending the meetings, and they were willing to help and encourage them in every way, but they did not think it was at all proper to invite them to join the Society, thus putting them on an equality with ourselves. Lucy and I maintained our ground, however, and the colored women were admitted.

I regret to be obliged, as a faithful chronicler of my anti-slavery experiences, to state that human nature changed little, for forty-two years later, in 1877, twelve years after the abolition of slavery, and many more years after the admission of colored children into the public schools of the city of Providence, my daughters and I were compelled, conscientiously, to resign our membership in the Rhode Island Women's Club, because that body refused admission to a highly respectable well-educated woman, solely on account of the color of her skin, although she had been a teacher of a colored school in that city for twenty-five years.

At one time, when we had an anti-slavery convention at Fall River, a large number of visitors dined at our house. Among them were the two New Bedford people, who had so shocked the sensibilities of the railroad officials at Taunton, and Charles Lenox Remond, a young colored anti-slavery orator. We had then in our house, in some useful capacity, a devoted Baptist woman, who usually sat at the family table. When dinner was ready, I asked her to join us. She replied, "No, I don't eat with niggers." When the dinner was over and the guests had retired to the parlor, I called her again. And again she answered, "No, I don't eat *with* niggers nor *after* 'em." Whether she went hungry that day, I never inquired.

In the year 1839, my husband and I removed with our family to Valley Falls, Rhode Island, bringing our anti-slavery principles with us. And, though he had been a consistent Friend from his youth up, and I remained clerk of Swanzey Monthly Meeting, until obliged to resign on account of our removal, the certificate they gave us to Providence Monthly Meeting, was deficient in respect to our standing, in that it omitted the usual acknowledgment that we were, "of orderly lives and conversation," and only declared our membership in the Society.

Our anti-slavery attitude soon put us under the ban of disapproval among Providence Friends. One day, soon after our removal, I was walking on a street in the city, when the leading Minister of Providence Monthly Meeting, overtook me, and greeted me very cordially. Walking beside me, he told me that he and his wife, also a

Minister, intended to call on us soon. I assured him a hearty welcome. And then I remembered that I had in my pocket an address to American Friends, on their inconsistent attitude toward the slavery question, by Joseph Sturge, an eminent English Friend, who had recently travelled in this country, and who had been an active laborer in the anti-slavery cause in England. I asked the Friend if he had seen it, and he said he had not, and I gave him the copy I had with me. His manner toward me changed at once, and he soon left me, and the proposed call was never made.

Within a few years following our removal to Rhode Island, many occurrences took place, which proved that the Society of Friends in the country was forgetful of its earlier record, and, like the other churches, had submitted to the domination of the slave-holding power. Uxbridge, Massachusetts, Monthly Meeting disowned Abby Kelley for anti-slavery lecturing, although they did so, ostensibly, on some frivolous charges, which had no real foundation in fact. Smithfield Monthly Meeting disowned my father, Arnold Buffum, on charges which he proved to them were false, and when he did so, and remonstrated against their threatened action, he was assured by the leading authority in the meeting, that it could "all be amicably settled, if he would give up this abolition lecturing," thus admitting that this was the offense for which he was to be disowned.

Several persons, in various parts of the country, were forcibly carried out of Friends' meetings for attempting therein to urge upon Friends the duty "to maintain faithfully their testimony against slavery," as their *Discipline* required. A few meeting houses in country places, had been opened for anti-slavery meetings; whereupon, our New England Yearly Meeting adopted a rule that no meeting house under its jurisdiction, should be opened except for meetings of our religious Society.

During those years, I could not help feeling a sense of grave responsibility for these unrighteous proceedings, so long as I remained a member of the Society, and my mind was deeply exercised concerning my duty in the matter. Other anti-slavery Friends thought it was best to remain in the Society, and strive to reform these abuses. But we were few in number; and the great body of Quakerism in the country was against us. Our lips were sealed in the Meetings, and out of Meetings we were in disgrace,—"despised and rejected."

One young Friend in Massachusetts had written a very earnest, open letter to Friends, in remonstrance for their pro-slavery position. He was universally condemned by all the powerful influences of the Society. Talking with one of the most influential members of our Yearly Meeting, who expressed strong condemnation of this young man's presumption, I said, "But is not what he says true?" And he replied, "Well, thee may be sure, it will certainly kill him as a Friend."

No belief in Papal infallibility was ever stronger in the Catholic mind, than was the assumption, not expressed in words, that the Society could do no wrong; and that, on this question of slavery, silence should be maintained; and no reproof, exhortation or entreaty against the pro-slavery attitude of the Society, should be tolerated. The claim of Friends, that the transaction of their Society affairs, should be under the immediate inspiration and guidance of the Holy Spirit, so beautifully set forth in many of their writings and sermons, as well as required in their *Discipline*, was sometimes perverted to authorize proceedings and actions which were far from being holy.

Finally, after a long struggle, I was compelled, in order to secure my own peace of mind, to resign my membership in the Society, to which, from my childhood, I had been devoutly attached. My husband remained in the Meeting, and the separation between the Wilburites and the Gurneyites soon occurring, he retired with the former, and preserved through the remainder of his life, unmolested and respected, his anti-slavery character; while I lost what little caste I held among the Friends, many of whom were near and dear to me by kin, and some of them by the nearer and dearer ties of life-long association and friendship. But, with my family cares and labor for the cause of the slave, and the associations it brought me, I had no time or inclination to worry over lost friendships; and the relief from responsibility for the pro-slavery attitude of the Society, was sufficient compensation for all I thus relinquished.

After coming to Rhode Island, our house became the resting place for the advocates of freedom for the slave, when travelling, or lecturing in this region, until the fetters which bound him were broken. William Lloyd Garrison, Wendell Phillips, Parker Pillsbury, Stephen S. Foster, Abby Kelley, Henry C. Wright, Charles Remond, Frederick Douglass, Charles and Cyrus Burleigh, Lucy Stone,

William Wells Brown and others of less note, were often our guests; and our children were born and bred in the atmosphere which these lovers of freedom helped to create in our household. The career of all these men and women should be written for the perusal of coming generations, as grand examples of noble, self-sacrificing manhood and womanhood, such as the world has seldom proved itself capable of producing.

When my own dear father and mother were with us, as they often were through their serene old age, the condemnation of slavery and the praises of liberty were always upon my father's lips. I can now seem to hear his rich, mellow voice, as he strolled about the house, reciting in the singsong Quaker fashion, the lines of Cowper—

> I would not have a slave to till my ground,
> To carry me, to fan me while I sleep,
> And tremble when I wake, for all the gold
> That sinews bought and sold have ever earned.
> No; dear as freedom is, and, in my heart's
> Just estimation, prized above all price,
> I would much rather be myself the slave,
> And wear the bonds, than fasten them on him.

or Montgomery's on the abolition of the slave trade by Great Britain—

> "Thy chains are broken,
>   Africa, be free!"
> Thus saith the Island—empress of the sea;
> Thus saith Britannia, O, ye winds and waves!
> Waft the glad tidings to the land of slaves,
> Proclaim on Guinea's coast, by Gambia's side,
> And far as Niger rolls his eastern tide,
> Through radiant realms, beneath the burning zone,
> Where Europe's curse is felt, her name unknown,
> Thus saith Britannia, empress of the sea,
> "Thy chains are broken, Africa, be free!"

And, other quotations of similar character. The songs of freedom from our young poet Whittier, then being issued from the press, my father was too old to commit to his already well-stored memory.

The *Liberator* and the *Anti-Slavery Standard* were our favorite newspapers; and *Uncle Tom's Cabin, The White Slave,* and other books of like purpose, were preferred before all others; while they shared with *Robinson Crusoe*, *The Swiss Family Robinson*, and other story books, the ordinary reading of our children in their early years.

As the anti-slavery agitation had created throughout the Northern States, an ever increasing sentiment against the iniquitous system, it could not fail to produce some effect on the South, occasionally of sympathy, but usually of bitter animosity, which was continually calling for the adoption of more stringent measures against Northern influence and interference. Travellers from the North, were subjected to the most rigid espionage, and sometimes, to personal indignity; one pious young man selling cottage Bibles, in Nashville, Tennessee, being publicly whipped, because, his wagon being searched, one copy of the book was found to be wrapped in a copy of the *Liberator*. A reward of five thousand dollars was offered, by the State of Georgia, for the body of William Lloyd Garrison; and it became entirely unsafe for any person who could not prove himself to be in favor of slavery, to travel in any State farther south than Pennsylvania and New Jersey. The slaves themselves, caught more and more the excitement of the agitation; and consequently, the number of escapes increased from year to year.

Although the holding of human beings in the Southern States, as slaves, and the right to recapture them in any part of the United States, were guaranteed by our national Constitution, it was found to be insufficient, inasmuch as it did not make resistance to their capture sufficiently penal. So, at the bidding of the slave-holding power, the famous Fugitive Slave Law was enacted by the Congress of 1850; Daniel Webster strongly defending its adoption on the seventh of March, in a speech in the United States Senate, which has made his name infamous in the reformed sentiment of New England.

Still, the anti-slavery spirit, grew and prospered, in proportion to the increase of the difficulties in its way. All through the States on the border line were Friends, who, in spite of the law, and the pro-slavery spirit around them, were ever ready to conceal, protect, and succor the fugitive until he could be sent to the British Dominion, where the slave-master could not reach him. Many were caught and returned to slavery, with all its horrors; still, one way and another, there were a good many who did reach Canada, and thus escape the vigilance of the mercenary human bloodhounds, who, as United States officers, were ever on the watch to make them their prey.

From the time of the arrival of James Curry at Fall River, and his departure for Canada, in 1839, that town became an important station on the so-called Underground Railroad. Slaves in Virginia would secure passage, either secretly or with consent of the captains, in small trading vessels, at Norfolk or Portsmouth, and thus be brought into some port in New England, where their fate depended on the circumstances into which they happened to fall. A few, landing at some towns on Cape Cod, would reach New Bedford, and thence be sent by an abolitionist there to Fall River, to be sheltered by Nathaniel B. Borden and his wife, who was my sister Sarah, and sent by them to my home at Valley Falls, in the darkness of night, and in a closed carriage, with Robert Adams, a most faithful Friend, as their conductor. Here, we received them, and, after preparing the for the journey, my husband would accompany them a short distance, on the Providence and Worcester railroad, acquaint the conductor with the facts, enlist his interest in their behalf, and then leave them in his care. They were then transferred at Worcester to the Vermont road, from which, by a previous general arrangement, they were received by a Unitarian clergyman named Young, and sent by him to Canada, where they uniformly arrived safely. I used to give them an envelope, directed to us, to be mailed in Toronto, which, when it reached us, was sufficient by its postmark to announce their safe arrival, beyond the baleful influence of the Stars and Stripes, and the anti-protection of the Fugitive Slave Law.

One evening, in answer to a summons at our door, we were met by Mr. Adams and a person, apparently in a woman's Quaker costume, whose face was concealed by a thick veil. The person, however, proved to be a large, noble-looking colored man, whose story was soon told. He had escaped from Virginia, bringing away with him a wife and child. Reaching New Bedford, he had found employment, which he had quietly pursued for eleven months. Being a very valuable piece of property (I think he was a blacksmith) his master had spared no pains in discovering his whereabouts; and, finally, traced him to New Bedford. Coming to Boston, he secured the services of a constable, and repaired to New Bedford, and went prowling round in search of his victim. But the colored people of that town discovering the purpose of the searchers, communicated with some of the few Abolitionists, and the man was hurried off to

Fall River, before the man-stealer had time to find him; and my sister Sarah and her husband Nathaniel Borden, dressed him in Quaker bonnet and shawl, and sent him off in the daylight, not daring to keep him till night, lest his master should follow immediately. He said he carried a revolver in his pocket, and, if his master should overtake him on the road, he would defend himself to the death of one of them, for no slave would he ever be again.

We sent him off on the early morning train, with fear and trembling; but had the happiness in a few days to learn of his safe arrival, of his having procured work, at once; and afterwards, that he had been joined by his wife and child. His master, after searching for him a whole day in New Bedford, had returned to Boston, very much disgusted with the indifference of the "Yankee Mudsills," as the lordly Southerners used to call New Englanders, to the misfortunes of the slave-holders; and wrote an indignant letter to a Boston pro-slavery newspaper, in which he complained bitterly of their want of sympathy and co-operation in his endeavor to recover his property. He said that, when he arrived in New Bedford, the bells were rung to announce his coming, and warn his slave, thus aiding in his escape; and that, every way, he was badly treated. The truth was, as we afterward learned, that he arrived at nine o'clock in the morning, just as the school-bells were ringing; and he understood this as a personal indignity.

Another time we were aroused about midnight, by the arrival of the good Friend Adams, with two young men, about twenty-four years old. They also were from Portsmouth, Virginia. They had each secured passage on a small trading vessel, bound for Wareham, Massachusetts, through the friendly interest of the colored steward, but without the knowledge of each other, or of the captain and crew of the vessel; and they were strangers to one another before their escape. The steward concealed one in the hold, and the other in his own berth, in the little cabin he had all to himself, and he carried them food in the night. They belonged to different masters, had each a wife and child, whom they said they would never have left, had they not learned that they were soon to be separated from them, and sold to the far south. So cruel was slavery in this country, less than forty years ago!

They were three days on the voyage. Before their arrival the steward told them of the presence of each other, and, as they would reach the port in the night, he requested them to remain concealed until three o'clock the next afternoon, at which time he would have left the vessel, as he would not engage for a return voyage. Then he instructed them how to proceed when they reached the shore. The rest of the story I will gave as nearly as I can, in the words of the man who occupied the steward's berth, premising, that it was then a time of extreme cold weather, about the last of Second Month; the ground being covered with ice and snow, and everything in a freezing condition.

"I was lyin' in de berth, while dey was unloadin' de cargo, an' I heered someone comin' toward de place where I lay. Dere had been a leak in de vessel, an' de Cap'n, he was searchin' round tryin' to find it. I covered myself wid de bedcloes, and flattened myself out like a plank, so I couldn't be seen. He come an' reached over me, feelin' along de side o' de vessel for de leak, and as he drew back his hand, it hit my head; an' den he stripped off de cloes an' dere I lay. Oh! den, I fell to beggin' an' prayin' him to let me go, but he went out widout speakin' a word, an' I heered him bolt two doors between me an' de deck. He meant to carry me back, but, God knows I couldn't go back dere no more, an' I alongside o' dat wharf. My coat, an' my hat, an' my shoes, was under dat berth, but I didn't stop for dem; and I bust open de two doors, reached de deck, an' jumped on de wharf, before dey had time to stop me. De Cap'n, he called to de men to seize me, but dey never moved; an' I run up de street as fast as I could. I found de colored woman and her son, de steward tole me to go to, an' dey took me in, an' de neighbors came in; an' dey warmed me, an' fed me, an' put cloes on me, an' I don't know what dey didn't do to me."

Then the poor, brave fellow told them there was another fugitive on board the vessel. And an old white man said he knew the captain, and he would go down and get him off. So, he went; it was dark, and he succeeded in finding the man in the hold, and brought him away without discovery; and the captain and sailors never knew that a second slave had been their passenger. But, the captain, hoping to set himself right with his patrons North and South, and make it safe for him to return to Virginia with his trade, went to New Bedford, and offered, through an advertisement, in a paper in that city, a reward of five hundred dollars, for the return to him of this young man who had so dexterously eluded his grasp. But he did not find him. He, with his fellow-traveller, was sitting by our fireside in Valley Falls while, with bolted doors and barred windows, we were hastily, with the help of one of our neighbors, fitting the two fugitives out with warmer clothing for their wintry journey northward. We had no time for anything more than to pick up what we could find, whether it fitted them or not, for we dared not keep them longer than was absolutely necessary. And when one of them put on a straight-collared, round-cut Quaker coat, which was much too large for him, the grotesqueness of his appearance caused them as well as ourselves much merriment, despite the sombre aspect of the situation.

Our neighbors did not all sympathize with our thus setting at nought the law of the land; which Daniel Webster, the great expounder, had so severely implored us to obey. One pious old deacon, in the Baptist Church, said, when the story got abroad, that we had no right thus to violate the law of the land. Had the slave-catchers come for those young men, we should not have opened our doors to them, and we should have done everything in our power, consistent with our peace principles, to prevent their capture. The consequences would, probably, have been serious to us, but we were prepared for whatever they might be, feeling sure, that we were obeying a higher and more imperative law. Our children and our servants entered heartily into our sentiment, although some of our Christian neighbors did not.

The fugitives reached Canada in safety, as the returned postmark soon informed us; but, whether they were ever joined by their wives and children, we never learned.

Another night, good Robert Adams aroused us with a carriage full—a woman, and three children. She had escaped from Maryland some time before, with her family, and established herself at Fall River, as a laundress; had made herself a home, and was doing well. Her eldest boy, of seventeen years, worked in a stable; and, after a while, had gone six miles away to work for a farmer. Soon after this, the same officer who arrested Anthony Burns, in Boston, arrived in Fall River, and was seen prowling around the neighborhood where colored people lived; and, especially and suspiciously, peering into the stable, where this woman's son had previously worked.

Always living in fear, in this so-called Land of Liberty, her excitement was extreme, when learning these facts. The friends of the slave, also, understood the good reasons for these fears, since the State of Massachusetts had so recently bowed to the slave-power, and in spite of the remonstrances and entreaties of the best citizens of the State, had cruelly sent back into slavery the man whom this miscreant had captured, for the reward it would bring him. So they hurried this woman off, with her three children, in the darkness of night to await, at Valley Falls, the disposal of her household effects and the bringing of her son from the farmer's. We kept them three or four days, in hourly fear and expectation of the arrival of the slave-catcher; our doors and windows fastened by day as well as by night, not daring to let our neighbors know who were our guests, lest some one should betray them. We told our children, all at that time under fourteen years of age, of the fine of one thousand dollars, and the imprisonment of six months that awaited us, in case the officer should come, and we should refuse to give these poor people up; and they heroically planned, how, in such an event, they would take care of everything; and, especially, that they would be good, and do just as we wished, during our absence.

The anti-slavery spirit pervaded our entire household during those eventful years. In this case, our faithful Irish servants declared that they would fight, before this woman and her children should be carried into slavery; and they were ready and willing to bear their share of the burdens incident to the occasion. So we waited, and kept our secret. On the third or fourth day, the boy arrived with money from the good friends at Fall River, and we sent them off, still fearing their capture on the road. The laws of the slave states condemned the children of a slave mother to follow her condition; so that, if the father was a free man, the children were all slaves. And, as the fathers were often white men, not seldom the slave-owners themselves, this was a very profitable arrangement; and frequently resulted in children being not only held as slaves, but in their being sold on the auction block by their own fathers. The beautiful quadroon girls, sold in the Southern markets, at enormous prices, carried in their veins the highest and noblest blood of the aristocracy of the Southern States, and, could their history be written, it would tell a tale of woe and sin and outrage.

In the case of the family of whom I write, the children were all boys; but, the youngest child, only a little over two years old, had evidently been born since the escape from slavery, and was nearly white; and the mother seemed to think he had more right to freedom than the others; and she said he should never be carried into slavery. So, when they were going off, I told her if they were caught on the train, to give him to some kind looking person, and request him to bring him to me, and I would keep him; and that relieved her, although, had they been caught it is not certain that she could have saved him thus. My husband accompanied them a part of the way to Worcester, and told their story to the conductor, who promised to see that they were safely started on the Vermont road. When he came back, he told Mr. Chace that the superintendent at Worcester said they should be taken care of, and if no train was going north soon enough to secure their safety, he would put on an extra train. The few days which followed were full of anxiety; but the envelope came back with the Toronto postmark, and the man-stealers lost their prey.

We had a few more experiences with escaped slaves which were of less interest; but in all of them we were surprised at the amount of intelligence and sharp-sightedness displayed by these victims of cruelty. And, indeed, they often appeared to have a keener sense of the difference between right and wrong then we would have supposed possible under the circumstances in which they lived; and which was far superior to that of the pro-slavery multitude which filled the churches and market places of New England. Of course it was the brightest and best who were capable of surmounting all the dangers and difficulties of escape from that terrible prison-house.

I remember only two instances in which we were deceived by impostors. One of these was when we kept, for ten days or more, an escaped burglar from the Auburn, New York, State Prison, a remarkably intelligent, gentlemanly, light-colored, handsome man, who assumed the rôle of a fugitive slave, to be protected from the officers of the law, and who was, when they finally caught him, declared by them to be one of the most desperate characters in the country. He made himself very interesting and agreeable to us during his stay, by his stories of Southern life, by his elegant manners, and especially by his great desire to learn our ideas about right and wrong, and for improvement of himself in all directions. He didn't do us any harm, and we hoped we did him some good. We never regretted that we had, for a short time, given him a glimpse of a life which was not criminal.

When the Liberty party was organized in 1840, with James G. Birney as its presidential candidate, and our own cousin Thomas Earle as its vice presidential candidate, my aged father, always looking for labor in some enterprise that promised immediate results, gave his support to that party, while we remained firm in the Garrisonian idea of no participation in a government that sanctioned slavery.

The summer and autumn of 1856, the year of the Fremont campaign, my parents spent with us. At a political meeting in our village of Valley Falls, on a warm, sultry evening, my father was speaking in favor of the anti-slavery candidate, and, in earnest tones, depicting the horrors of slavery and the blessings of freedom, when, suddenly, he fainted, and fell prostrate on the platform. We hastened to his side, supposing he was dying, and I remember well, how, in my distress, I felt great satisfaction in the fact that the last utterance from his lips, was the grand word, "Liberty." I knew, if he could, he would have chosen that. He recovered, however, and lived several years after, to bear further testimony in the slave's behalf; but not, like Garrison, to see slavery abolished.

The campaign of that year was a very exciting one; and our children entered heartily into it; and when the watchwords of the parties were flying in the air, and floating from every flagstaff, they prepared, also, to display their several predilections. While two of my boys, Samuel and Edward, aged thirteen and seven years, manufactured and swung from the top of the well-house, the Stars and the Stripes, with "Fremont and Freedom," in flaming letters, Arnold, aged eleven, quietly constructed his flag, all by himself, and ascending to the top of our house, swung it out upon the breeze, bearing, in brilliant color, the motto of the *Liberator*, "No Union With Slave-holders." I think our little girls sympathized with all their brothers, and rejoiced in the waving of both the flags.

When John Brown attempted to free the slaves in 1859 by his attack at Harper's Ferry, our family was stirred by strong emotions. On the dark day, when the grand, but mistaken old man, was hung on a Virginian gallows, a solitary strip of black drapery on our door reminded our neighbors that, with us, it was a day of mourning.

A younger sister of mine, Rebecca Buffum Spring, lived then at Eagleswood, near Perth Amboy, New Jersey. Like all of our family she and her husband Marcus Spring were active in the Anti-Slavery cause. Her husband was a very wealthy New York merchant and they had for years used their resources in aiding the cause of the Negroes.

On October 17, 1859, came the startling news that men, led by John Brown, had attacked the Federal arsenal at Harper's Ferry, Virginia. There had been loss of life and the raiders had been captured and imprisoned.

My sister was deeply agitated at the news for she felt that John Brown and his men had, although unwisely, taken the first positive step toward ending the impossible conditions under which the country was laboring.

On November 2, 1859, the Circuit Court of Jefferson County, Virginia, pronounced upon John Brown and his men, the sentence of death. Lydia Maria Child, the well loved Boston Abolitionist, had requested permission of Governor Wise of Virginia, to visit the condemned men, and had seen them.

When Rebecca heard of this visit she felt that she also must do everything in her power to comfort and help the captives. Although she had never met John Brown she was touched by his blind devotion to the Negro, his lack of malice, his honesty of purpose, and his high courage. She felt that she must go to see him and try to ease his path, which all knew, was now only to death.

At first, after the Harper's Ferry raid, Virginians and Southerners generally felt that it was the wild thought of one unbalanced brain, or at most the work of one fanatic representing only a small group of extremists. Governor Wise and the people of Virginia therefore treated the prisoners with considerable magnanimity.

By November 5, however, an entirely different feeling pervaded the state, for in the week since the raid the Northern press had adopted John Brown as the champion of freedom and its columns were filled with burning denunciation of Virginia and its Governor. A leading Northern daily paper wrote that Pontius Pilate was gentle in comparison to Governor Wise. Ministers of the gospel throughout the North spoke in like vein and the mail of the governor was filled with denunciation and abuse and threats of personal revenge.

Sentiment in Virginia changed from contemptuous annoyance to real and bitter hate, and the feeling became widespread that Northerners as a whole were antagonistic and furiously determined to wreak vengeance on the officials and body politic of the State.

It was just at this time that my sister Rebecca decided to go to see John Brown. Accompanied only by her young son, Edward, nineteen years old, she left Eagleswood on November fourth, for Charlestown.

When the slave-holding power ushered in the rebellion, by firing on Fort Sumter, the Abolitionists, hoping to avert the horrors of a protracted civil war, held meetings throughout New England, to arouse the North to a sense of the necessity to emancipate the slaves, as the only method by which peace could be restored. But, so blind were the masses of the people, that the pro-slavery spirit was renewedly aroused thereby, and mobs and outrages once more assailed the truest friends of the nation.

In our village of Valley Falls we had a meeting appointed for a Sunday evening, to be addressed by Henry C. Wright, one of the firmest friends of humanity this country has ever known. A few pro-slavery politicians encouraged some rude fellows of the baser sort, to prepare themselves to break up the meeting. Anti-Slavery friends came from Providence and Pawtucket; and, accompanied by the speaker, we all walked over to the hall, rumors of the intended disturbance having reached our ears. As we approached, we saw rough looking men standing about, and as soon as Mr. Wright began to speak a crowd of them entered and seated themselves. They hissed and groaned and stamped, until, after several vain attempts to make himself heard, he was compelled to give up the struggle, and in the midst of great noise and confusion, we passed out, accompanied by the mob. We Abolitionists formed a solid phalanx around our speaker, the children among us, while we walked quietly the distance to our house, the mob following close upon us, with yells and shouts and threats of violence, and the occasional hurling of a stone, thus proving their intention to do us harm. When we reached our gate, they halted; and when we entered the house, they dispersed, apparently wearied with their evil work, or, perhaps, ashamed and awed by our non-resistant attitude.

Then came another day to the anti-slavery workers. As, through all the preceding years, we had circulated petitions to Congress, for the abolition of slavery in the District of Columbia, and the Territories, we now began to petition the President, Abraham Lincoln, to issue a proclamation of emancipation, as the only means of staying the tide of bloodshed and distress which threatened our country with destruction; and, as an act of tardy justice to the bruised and tortured victims of our national cruelty. His first reply to such petitions was that he intended to put down the rebellion. If he could do it without abolishing slavery, he should.

And so the war went on; millions of treasure were wasted, young manhood bled on the battle field, and mothers' hearts were rent and torn. And when, after years of strife and bloodshed, the President did finally, as a military necessity, issue the proclamation of emancipation, we rejoiced with exceeding great joy; and made no resistance to the honor it gave him, as the emancipator. And when he was stricken down by the assassin's hand, no more sorrowing mourners than we wept over the sad event.

In the confusion and difficulty that followed this sudden overthrow of slavery, which threw the emancipated slaves, without any resources, upon their own responsibility, much remained to be done to save them from starvation, nakedness and homelessness. The people of the Northern States were aroused to great activity in their behalf; and a widespread sympathy and generosity were extended toward them. But none except the long-tried Abolitionists saw the necessity of all removal of race prejudice and the establishment of the principle of a common humanity. The public schools of Rhode Island had, some years before this, after a severe and protracted struggle, been opened to colored children. And yet, about the beginning of the war, a lad of rare excellence and attainments was refused an examination for admission to Brown University, on account of the color of his skin.

In the year 1865 while the Friends of Rhode Island were contributing liberally, and working devotedly, for the relief of the freedmen, the Yearly Meeting committee having charge of the Friends School in Providence, refused admission to a boy and girl, the children of a respectable colored physician of Boston, who was to be sent by a philanthropic association to look after the welfare of the emancipated slaves in New Orleans, and who wished to place his children in a good school during his absence. The committee were solicited to show their interest in the freedmen by receiving these motherless children into the school, but they replied that "the time had not yet come to take such a step," and our appeals fell on deaf ears.

My own convictions, long since established, were confirmed by these and other similar experiences, that it is not right for me to give any countenance or support to charitable or educational institutions maintained exclusively for colored people. The colored people are here, by no choice of their own—members of our body politic; and the sooner they are admitted to all the privileges of citizenship, and estimated solely by their merits and qualifications, the better for all concerned. It is a baneful policy to undertake to support two distinct nationalities or municipalities in one commonwealth, or two distinct social fabrics, on any basis except that of mental and moral fitness.

All these experiences were an important feature in the education of our children of which, circumstances being as they were, I would by no means have deprived them. For there is no better influence toward the building up of a strong virtuous manhood and womanhood, than the espousal in early life of some great humanitarian cause as a foundation. By such preparation men and women are made ready to take up all questions which concern the advancement of mankind. The slavery of the black man is abolished, the shackles have fallen from his limbs and he is crowned with the diadem of citizenship. It is too late to become an Abolitionist now but in the process of overthrowing one great wrong there is always laid bare some other wrong, which requires for its removal the same self-sacrificing spirit, the same consecration to duty, as accomplished the preceding reform. So it has ever been.

In the progress of the anti-slavery movement experience revealed the great injustice, the detriment to human welfare, of the subordinate, disfranchised condition of woman. Every step in that great reform was impeded by the inequality that depressed and degraded her. And these experiences were to the Abolitionists, in this, as in other directions, a liberal education. So, when the crime of slaveholding was overcome, they became the leaders in the women's suffrage cause, their children, as a rule, following in their footsteps, in the broader, more world-wide reformation, than was the conflict for the overthrow of slavery. For, although we have not the chain, the lash and the auction block in their literal sense to complain of, there is enough that is unjust and degrading in the condition of women to convince us that the work to which this generation of reformers is called, is of far wider significance to the progress of all mankind than was the anti-slavery struggle. Blessed are they, who, when some great cause calls to them, "Come, follow me," are found ready to obey the Divine summons.

• 5 •

A Visit to John Brown in 1859

by Rebecca Buffum Spring

When I decided I must go to Harper's Ferry to see John Brown my husband, Marcus, entreated me against it. The way was full of dangers, he urged, and I could never get there. I answered, "We have talked against slavery all these years. Now somebody has done something. These men have risked their lives. I must go." "It would kill me," he replied; and so I gave it up. Later, while on a trip to New York, he sent this message back:

"Mrs. Child has gone to see the prisoners, by permission of the governor of Virginia; what a pity you didn't go with her!" Taking this for consent, before he returned home, my young son and I were on our way south.

At Baltimore I must ask my road, but at first I must find one of whom it seemed safe to inquire. Then, while still in the station, I noticed a gentleman speaking to a lady in the Friends' manner. It so happened that these two shared a carriage with me going to the hotel, and so I asked about trains for Harper's Ferry. Presently, in the hotel parlor, the gentleman came to me with: "They say Mrs. Child has permission to visit the prisoners," adding, with a twinkle of the eyes, "She'd better stay at home and mind her own business!"

"Perhaps," I answered, "she thinks, as I do, that when men fight and hurt each other, women should go to take care of them."

"I guess thee is going to see John Brown," he retorted shrewdly.

"I have linen for bandages," said I, "and a bottle of arnica, in my trunk." Then he laid out our whole journey until we should be safe in the Carter House in Charlestown, and gave me the name of a Quaker resident of that place.

We reached the Wager House, at Harper's Ferry, at about nine o'clock; and as the night was cold, drew near the fire. A gentleman called to see a lady staying at the hotel. They sat directly behind my chair. The lady remarked to her visitor that the ladies in the hotel felt like prisoners since the raid (October 16–17), the streets being full of soldiers and men in arms. She told of a night when they were awakened by fearful cries and the firing of guns. They had thought it an insurrection of the slaves, she said, and that they should all be murdered. She told how the citizens in the fight of the seventeenth had brought a wounded raider into that very room; and how the sister of the landlord stood before the captive and begged them to leave him to the law, and how, as she would not let them kill him there, they dragged him out and one of them killed him on the bridge, close by. And she said, "I wanted to kill them all."

"Who killed him?" I asked, starting to my feet. "How cowardly to kill a wounded man!"

The lady and all the people hurried away. Only the gentleman stopped to answer:

"Madam, it was one of our citizens. He would not have done it, but our mayor had been shot down in the street." Then he, too, left.

We took the morning train for Charlestown, the county-seat, eight miles from Harper's Ferry. Many rough-looking men were hanging about the station there, and I was thankful that I had no need to ask questions, but had only to give my checks to a porter and walk up to the Carter House, the principal inn of the place.

There the courteous landlord could not tell me where Mrs. Child was stopping, and even stated that no such lady had arrived. I insisted, and added that I came to join her. As he could tell me nothing of her,

however, I set out to find Friend Howells, to whom I had been recommended by my Baltimore acquaintance. He lived at the other end
of the village. The streets were filled with formidable-looking men,
but no one spoke us; yet I was glad to reach my destination. A servant conducted us through a hall to the dining-room, where several
people were at table. The Friend received us very graciously and asked
us to dine.

"I met thy friend Edward Stabler in Baltimore," said I, "who
told me thee could give me important information. Can thee tell
me where Mrs. Child is?"

"Mrs. Child?" he said.

"The lady who has come here from Boston, by permission of
the governor, to see the prisoners."

The Friend flew into a most unfriendly rage. Starting to his feet, he
shouted: "I have nothing, and will have nothing to do with these things."

"Neither have I, but I thought I might ask for my friend in a
Friend's house without giving offense," I replied.

"I have nothing to do with it. Let her stay in her own country
and mind her own business."

"I even thought she might be in this house."

"I wouldn't receive her if she came."

"I rather think John Woolman would."

"I don't care what John Woolman would. I know David Howells
wouldn't."

I reminded him of some of the principles of the Friends, but he
only raged the more. So, stepping up the one step into the hall, I said:
"Peace be to this house," then turned and walked to the entrance.

He followed, muttering about dangerous times. When the light
came in through the open door I was shocked to see the change in
the man. He trembled, his lips were blue, his face twitched ner-
vously. I was sorry for him; and my way seemed dark.

The street, on the return, was still more crowded with sinister-
looking men. When we reached the hotel, I asked for the landlord;
but as soon as he came the room filled with men. He thought I would
better come out on a back piazza. But instantly that, too, was crowded,
while listeners pressed in every door and window. I said:

"I went to see the Quaker man, and he was cross as a bear. And
I can't find Mrs. Child."

"Why don't you go to see Brown's physician?" asked the land-lord. "He is a gentleman and will be civil to you."

To the physician's house we went. The servant said he was home, and a kind looking gentleman came and assured me that Mrs. Child was not in town. After a little talk, he explained that he was not the doctor, who was too ill to see me.

"You have answered as the doctor—who are you?"

"I am a justice of the peace."

"Then open the prison door for me."

"Only Sheriff Campbell can do that." He advised me to write to the sheriff, and actually walked up the street with me. Passing the prison, he pointed out a kind-looking man of powerful frame, standing on the platform before the door, as the jailer, Avis. At my request, the justice called Avis down, but instantly there was such a rush of men, thrusting their faces between us, that we could not talk; so Avis said that he would call at the hotel to see me. He came and from that time did all that he could to enable me to effect my wish, even using some strong words about it. Mean-while, I had sent to the sheriff a note which, in due season, brought me the following reply:

November 6, 1859

Mrs. Spring: Dear Madam—I received your note late last night requesting an interview with Capt. Brown. I am sorry I cannot grant your request; public opinion is very much excited by your coming here, and our object is to allay that excitement. I also understand from Capt. Brown that he does not wish to see you, or any one else. My responsibility is very great. If anything should occur in conse-quence of my granting you, or any one else, an interview, I should be censured by the whole community. I must therefore deny your request.

Yours respectfully,

J.W. Campbell, *Sheriff*

While waiting for the reply I had sent toilet articles and other comforts to Capt. Brown, by my son, until the landlord said it was dangerous for him again to go through the mob to the prison. When I told the landlord that the sheriff had refused my request, he advised me to see George Sennott, the Boston lawyer, of counsel for Brown and his men, who was then in the hotel. I sent for him, and here at last found a true friend and helper. On the second day, Sunday, November 6, of my stay in Charlestown, Mr. Sennott obtained from the judge of the court an order for my admission to the prison at three o'clock, and he brought a message from Capt. Brown that he should be glad to see me.

I had not dared to leave the house for fear of losing just such a chance. We now decided to take a walk. With my son I walked to a grove of forest trees, where I gathered leaves of rich autumn tints and fastened them together with thorns. Returning to the hotel, I told the landlord that I had now permission to enter the prison and asked him to give me a half-opened rose that I saw in the garden. He answered: "Yes, that, or anything else."

At the hour appointed we were admitted to the guardroom in the prison to wait for the jailer, then engaged in the court room across the street. Presently I saw men bringing a man, apparently dying, from the court house into the prison. This was Aaron D. Stevens, Brown's lieutenant, desperately wounded in the Harper's Ferry raid. He had fainted several times during his trial, and the judge had ordered him returned to his cell. Avis, the jailer, accompanied him, and I was glad to think my waiting over, but Avis said that he must forthwith return to the court house with Cook, another of Capt. Brown's imprisoned men.

"Will you go back to the hotel, or wait for me here?" he asked.

"I will wait here," said I.

Some dozen men occupied the guardroom. Their talk was rough. The stove-heated air was suffocating, and it was not a pleasant half-hour for my son and me. At last Avis returned and led us into the prison room. On one bed lay John Brown, on the other, Stevens. Mr. Brown attempted to rise, but could not stand. I gave him the rose, which he laid on his pillow. I looked for a nail on which to hang my leaves. Mr. Brown said they had taken out every nail. The window had strong iron bars; behind the bars I put the bright leaves. He looked pleased, and his wife told me afterwards that I could not have carried him a better gift, for he loved the woods. We drew our chairs near Mr. Brown's bed; the jailer sat on a bench back in a corner; I unrolled some worsted work and began to knit; Brown looked gratified and was inclined to talk. First he spoke of Avis's kindness—"If he had been my father or brother he could not have been kinder"; again, soon after—"I don't think they can do anything better with me now, than hang me."

"I do not know what weakness may come over me; but I do not believe I shall deny my Lord and Master, Jesus Christ, and I should if I denied my principles against slavery. Why, I preach against it all the time. Capt. Avis knows I do."

"Yes," said Avis.

Brown went on: "I have attempted to carry out my faith by works. I feel no regret for what I have done; and I cannot now serve the cause I love so well better than to die for it. The sentence they have passed upon me did not disturb me in the least. It is not the first time I have looked death in the face." Then he said laughing: "I am more afraid of meeting ladies and gentlemen in company than of meeting men with guns."

"I want to ask you one question," said I, "not for myself, but for others. In what you did at Harper's Ferry were you actuated by a spirit of revenge?" Brown started, looked surprised, then replied:

"No, not in all the wrongs done to me and to my family in Kansas did I ever have a feeling of revenge."

The shyness that I believe he felt in the presence of strangers was wearing off. He spoke several times to my son and looked at him tenderly. He was becoming more cordial and communicative when a loud voice called, "Avis!" It was Sheriff Campbell. The crowd had become impatient and threatened violence if I were allowed to stay longer. The sheriff, alarmed, twice called the jailer. Avis hastened out and returned instantly with the verdict that I must leave. I shook hands with Brown on parting. "The Lord will bless you for coming here," said he.

The great, tall sheriff opened the door and hurried out a little woman and a boy into the face of a furious mob of the worst-looking men I ever saw. We stood for a moment on the little platform at the top of the steps, and looked down over a sea of angry eyes and clenched and threatening hands and I did not feel afraid! I, who dare not pass a cow and who have such a terror of great dogs, was so uplifted in spirit that I had lost all feeling of fear and walked through the mob, which opened just wide enough to let us pass, without thinking of the mob at all. I believe I was safer because I was not afraid. It was when Peter was afraid that he began to sink. It is good sometimes to get a glimpse of the power within us.

Mr. Sennott brought me constant news of Capt. Brown. He improved steadily. Seeing nothing more that I could hope to do, I was intending to return home, when on November 8th Mr. Sennott desired me to see Mr. Brown again, in order to take a message from him to his wife, then in Philadelphia. I sent for Judge Parker, presiding judge of the Circuit Court, then in session, who not only granted me the permission I asked, but gave me his arm to the prison.

What a different man I now found! Capt. Brown was sitting at a table, writing. He looked well; his hair, that had been matted with dried clots of blood, was washed and brushed. Thrown up from his brow, it made a soft white halo around his head. His high white forehead expressed a sort of glory. He looked like an inspired old prophet. He had just finished a letter to his wife and children. This he requested me to read and take to his wife, to whom he sent many messages. The last farewell was a silent one. Our hearts were too full for words. Stevens lay on his bed, apparently dying, but his great eyes shone, and his face was full of joy.

Capt. Brown stood by the table as I left the room—a commanding figure, the white halo about his high head, on his face a look of peace. For twenty years he had believed himself divinely called to free the slaves. He had tried and failed. The slave power seemed stronger than ever; his little band of earnest young men were scattered, dead, or imprisoned, and he himself was condemned to die on the scaffold. But his faith never flinched.

On November 24th John Brown wrote to me, "I am always grateful for anything you do or write. You have laid me and my family under many and great obligations."

John Brown died on December 2nd and four of his men on December 16th. Aaron D. Stephens and Hazlitt were sentenced to die in March, 1860. I wrote many letters to these boys that winter and sent them many boxes of food and clothing.

I urged Colonel Thomas Wentworth Higginson to make a determined effort to rescue Stevens and Hazlitt, and he later told me that my pleadings had persuaded him to make the attempt. He and Captain James Montgomery and a group of brave fellows actually went to Harper's Ferry and endeavored to plan a successful attack on the prison. They soon decided however that such effort would be useless and only insure their own death.

Later, when the two last members of John Brown's party had been hung, my husband and I sent for the bodies and had them brought to our home at Eagleswood. The funeral services were held there and the boys were buried in our ground.

• 6 •

A Slave's Escape

by James Curry, As Told to
Elizabeth Buffum Chace, Written in 1839

Perhaps the most interesting story that I am able to tell regarding the escape of a slave in which my family and I were able to be of great assistance is that of James Curry who was one of the first to go through Fall River and from there to Canada. I will write his story as he told it many times to me but since it is rather long, I will not attempt to give it in his own vernacular:

I was born in Person County, North Carolina. My master's name was Moses Chambers. My mother was the daughter of a white man and a slave woman. She, with her brother, were given, when little children, to my master's mother, soon after her marriage, by her father. Their new master and mistress were both drunkards, and possessed very little property beside these two slaves. My mother was treated very cruelly. O! I cannot tell you how dreadful her treatment was while she was a young girl. It is not proper to be written; but the treatment of females in slavery is very dreadful.

When she was about fifteen years old, she attempted to run away. She got about fifteen miles, and stopped at the house of a poor white woman, with the intention of staying there four weeks, until her brother, who had a wife near there, came down to see her, which he did once in four weeks. She could not bear to go farther without hearing from her mother, and giving her intelligence of herself. She also wished to procure herself some clothes, as she was very destitute. At the end of three weeks, there came in a white man, who knew and arrested her, and returned her to her master. She soon afterwards married a slave in the neighborhood.

Her mistress did not provide her with clothes, and her husband obtained for her a wheel, which she kept in her hut, for the purpose of spinning in the night, after her day's work for her cruel mistress was done. This her mistress endeavored to prevent, by keeping her spinning in the house until twelve or one o'clock at night. But she would then go home, and, fixing her wheel in a place made in the floor to prevent it making a noise, she would spin for herself, in order that she might be decently clad in the daytime. Her treatment continued so bad, that she, with her sister Ann, who was the slave of her mistress's sister, resolved to run away again. Her sister had a husband, who concluded to go too; and then my mother informed her husband, and they all four started together.

Not knowing any better, they went directly south. After travelling two or three nights, Ann's husband thought they could travel safely by day, and so they walked on in the morning. They had got but a little way, when they met a white man, who stopped and asked them, "Are you travellers?" They answered, "Yes, sir." "Are you free?" "Yes, sir." "Have you free papers?" "Yes, sir." (They got some person to furnish them before they started.) "Well," said he, "go back to the next village, and we will have them examined." So he took them before a magistrate, who examined the papers and said, "These won't do." He then said to the girls, "Girls, we don't doubt that *you* are free, and if you choose, you may go on; but these boys you have stolen from their masters, and they must go to jail." At that time, before the laws against emancipation were passed, bright mulattoes, such as these girls were, would be allowed to pass along the road unmolested, but now they could not. The girls, being unwilling to part with their husbands, went to jail with them, and being advertised, their masters came after them in a few days. This ended my mother's running away. Having young children soon, it tied her to slavery.

Two or three years after this, she was separated from her husband by the removal of her master to the South. The separation of the slaves in this way is little thought of. A few masters regard their union as sacred, but where one does, a hundred care nothing about it. I knew a member of a Methodist church, who was making up a drove of slaves to send by his two sons to Alabama. He had one girl, whom he intended to send in this drove, whose husband belonged to another man. While preparing to depart, one of his sons said to him, "It is wrong thus to separate man and wife." The father raved at him, in great fury, saying, "Do you talk to me about *a nigger's wife?*" The drove was sent off, and in two or three months, the other son wrote to his father, that he who had thus compassionated the Negro's sufferings was dead, and before he returned, his mother died also.

My uncle learned the hatter's trade, and being very smart, he supported his drunken master and mistress. He used to make hats, and then go off and sell them, and return the money to his master. But they spent so much that they got in debt, and were obliged to sell the slaves, who were purchased by their son, Moses Chambers. After this, my mother was married to a free colored man, named Peter Burnet, who was my father. When they had been married about two years, he travelled south with a white man, as his servant, who sold him into slavery, and she never saw him again. After a few years, she married a slave belonging to her master, and has since had six children. She gave to each of her children two names, but we were called by only one. It is not common for slaves to have more than one name, but my mother was a proud-spirited woman, and she gave her children two. She was a very good and tender mother. She never made a public profession of religion, but she always tried to do right, and taught her children to know right from wrong. When I was a little child, she taught me to know my Maker, and that we should all die, and if we are good, we should be happy.

From my childhood until I was sixteen years old, I was brought up a domestic servant. I played with my master's children, and we loved one another like brothers. This is often the case in childhood, but when the young masters and misses get older, they are generally sent away from home to school, and they soon learn that slaves are not companions for them. When they return, the love of power is cultivated in their hearts by their parents, the whip is put into their hands, and they soon regard the Negro in no other light than as a slave. My master's oldest son was six months older than I.

He went to a day school, and as I had a great desire to learn to read, I prevailed on him to teach me. My mother procured me a spelling book. Before Nat Turner's insurrection, a slave in our neighborhood might buy a spelling or hymn book, but now he cannot. I got so I could read a little, when my master found it out, and forbade his son to teach me any more. As I had got the start, however, I kept on reading and studying and from that time till I came away, I always had a book somewhere about me, and if I got an opportunity, I would be reading in it. Indeed, I have a book now, which I brought all the way from North Carolina.

I borrowed a hymn book, and learned the hymns by heart. My uncle had a Bible, which he lent me, and I studied the Scriptures. When my master's family were all gone away on the Sabbath, I used to go into the house and get down the great Bible, and lie down in the piazza, and read, taking care, however, to put it back before they returned. There I learned that it was contrary to the revealed will of God, that one man should hold another as a slave. I had always heard it talked among the slaves, that we ought not to be held as slaves; that our forefathers and mothers were stolen from Africa, where they were free men and free women. But in the Bible I learned that, "God hath made of one blood all nations of men to dwell on all the face of the earth."

While I worked in the house and waited upon my mistress, she always treated me kindly, but to other slaves, who were as faithful as I was, she was very cruel. At one time, there was a comb found broken in a cupboard, which was worth about twenty-five or thirty-seven-and-a-half cents. She suspected a little girl, nine or ten years old, who served in the house, of having broken it. She took her in the morning, before sunrise, into a room, and calling me to wait upon her, had all the doors shut. She tied her hands, and then took her frock up over her head, and gathered it up in her left hand, and with her right commenced beating her naked body with bunches of willow twigs. She would beat her until her arm was tired, and then thrash her on the floor, and stamp on her with her foot, and kick her, and choke her to stop her screams. O! it was awful! and I was obliged to stand there and see it, and to go and bring her the sticks. She continued this torture until ten o'clock, the family waiting breakfast meanwhile. She then left whipping her; and that night, she herself was so lame that one of her daughters was obliged to undress her. The poor child never recovered. A white swelling came from the bruises on one of her legs, of which she died in two or three years. And my mistress was soon after called by her great Master to give her account.

Before her death, my mistress used to clothe her people with coarse, common clothing. She had been dead eleven years when I came away. She died in October, and in the following spring, my master bought about one hundred yards of coarse tow and cotton, which he distributed among the slaves. After this, he provided no clothing for any of his slaves, except that I have known him in a few instances to give a pair of thoroughly worn-out pantaloons to one. They worked in the night upon their little patches of ground, raising tobacco and food for hogs, which they were allowed to keep, and thus obtained clothes for themselves. These patches of ground were little spots they were allowed to clear in the woods, or cultivate upon the barrens, and after they got them nicely cleared, and under good cultivation, the master took them away, and the next year they must take other uncultivated spots for themselves.

There were on this plantation nine men, and eight out of this nine were always as decently clad as any slaves in that part of the country; and each had a better suit for Sunday. The ninth was a young fellow, who had not been taught by his mother to take care of himself, but he was fast improving when I came away. It was to him that my master gave the worn-out pantaloons. My stepfather felled trees in the woods, and built for his family a commodious log house. With my mother's assistance, it was furnished with two comfortable beds, chairs, and some other articles of furniture. His children were always comfortably and decently clothed. I knew him, at one time, to purchase for my mother a cloak, and a gown, a frock for each of my two sisters, two coats for two brothers younger than myself, and each of them a hat, all new and good, and all with money earned in the time allowed him for sleep.

My mother was cook in the house for about twenty-two years. She cooked for from twenty-five to thirty-five, taking the family and the slaves together. The slaves ate in the kitchen. After my mistress's death, my mother was the only woman kept in the house. She took care of my master's children, some of whom were then quite small, and brought them up. One of the most trying scenes I ever passed through, when I would have laid down my life to protect her if I had dared, was this: after she had raised my master's children, one of his daughters, a young girl, came into the kitchen one day, and for some trifle about the dinner, she struck my mother, who pushed her away, and she fell on the floor. Her father was not at home. When he came, which was while the slaves were eating in the kitchen, she told him about it. He came down, called my mother out, and with a hickory rod, he beat her fifteen or twenty strokes, and then called his daughter and told her to take her satisfaction of her, and she did beat her until she was satisfied. O! it was dreadful, to see the girl whom my poor mother had taken care of from her childhood, thus beating her, and I must stand there, and did not dare to crook my finger in her defence.

My mother's labor was very hard. She would go to the house in the morning, take her pail upon her head, and go away to the cow-pen, and milk fourteen cows. She then put on the bread for the family breakfast, and got the cream ready for churning, and set a little child to churn it, she having the care of from ten to fifteen children, whose mothers worked in the field. After clearing away the family breakfast, she got breakfast for the slaves; which consisted of warm corn bread and buttermilk, and was taken at twelve o'clock. In the meantime, she had beds to make, rooms to sweep, and many other duties. Then she cooked the family dinner, which was simply plain meat, vegetables and bread. Then the slaves' dinner was to be ready at from eight to nine o'clock in the evening. It consisted of cornbread, or potatoes, and the meat which remained of the master's dinner, or one herring apiece. At night she had the cows to milk again. There was little ceremony about the master's supper, unless there was company. This was her work day by day.

Then in the course of the week, she had the washing and ironing to do for her master's family, who, however, were clothed very simply, and for her husband, seven children and herself.

She would not get through to go to her log cabin until nine or ten o'clock at night. She would then be so tired, that she could scarcely stand; but she would find one boy with his knee out, and another with his elbow out, a patch wanting here, and a stitch there, and she would sit down by her lightwood fire, and sew and sleep alternately, often till the light began to streak in the east; and then lying down, she would catch a nap, and hasten to the toil of the day. Among the slave children were three little orphans, whose mothers, at their death, committed them to the care of my mother. One of them was a babe. She took them and treated them as her own. The master took no care about them. She always took a share of the cloth she had provided for her own children, to cover these little friendless ones. She would sometimes ask the master to procure them some clothes, but he would curse them and refuse to do it. We would sometimes tell her, that we would let the master clothe them, for she had enough to do for her own children. She replied, "Their master will not clothe them, and I cannot see them go naked; I have children and I do not know where their lot may be cast; I may die and leave them, and I desire to do by these little orphans, as I should wish mine to be done by."

After I was sixteen, I was put into the field to work in the spring and summer, and in the autumn and winter, I worked in the hatter's shop with my uncle. We raised on the plantation, principally, tobacco, some cotton, and some grain. We commenced work as soon as we could see in the morning, and worked from that time until twelve o'clock before breakfast, and then until dark, when we had our dinner, and hastened to our night work for ourselves. We were not driven as field slaves generally are, and yet when I hear people here say they work as hard as the slaves, I can tell them from experience, they know nothing about it. And even if they did work as hard, there is one striking difference. When they go home at night, they carry to their families the wages of their daily labor; and then they have the night for rest and sleep. Whereas, the slave carries to his family at night, only a weary body and a sick mind, and all he can do for them is done during the hours allowed him for sleep.

A slave, who was hired during one summer by Thomas Maguhee, a rich slave-holder in our neighborhood, soon after his return, passed with me, one day, near a field on his plantation. Pointing to it, he said, "I never saw blood flow anywhere as I've seen it flow in that field. It flows there like water. When I went there to work, I was a *man*, but now, I am a *boy*. I could then carry several bushels on my shoulder, but now I cannot lift one to it." So very hard had he been worked. When arranging the slaves for hoeing in the field, the over-seer takes them, one at a time, and tries their speed, and places them accordingly in the row, the swiftest first, and so on. Then they commence, and all must keep up with the foremost.

This Thomas Maguhee used to walk into his field, with his hat close down on his head, and holding his cane over his shoulder. When he came up to the poor slaves, as they were tugging at their hoes, he would call out, "Boys!" When they must all raise their hats and reply simultaneously, "Sir." "Move your hoes." They would spring forward and strive to increase their speed to the utmost; but presently he would call out again, "Boys!" Again the hats were raised as they answered, "Sir." "I told you to move your hoes, and you haven't moved them yet. I have twice to threat and once to fall." (That is, if you do not move faster, I shall knock you down.) Now the poor creatures must make their last effort, he would set his hat on the top of his head, take down his cane, set his arms akimbo and strut through the field.

Judge Duncan Cameron was a very rich man, who lived in Raleigh, and owned a plantation in our neighborhood. He used to carry a large cane, and if he met a Negro on the road, and he did not raise his hat and bow to him, he would beat him with his cane. It is the custom, whenever a white man meets a colored man in the road, to call out to him, no matter what his age may be, "Hulloa, boy, whom do you belong to?"

From my childhood, the desire for freedom reigned predomi-nant in my breast, and I resolved, if I was ever whipped after I became a man, I would no longer be a slave. When I was a lad, my master's uncle came one day to see him, and as I was passing near them, the old man took hold of me and asked my master if this was one of Lucy's boys. Being told that I was, he said, "Well, his father was a free man and perhaps when he gets to be a man, he'll be wanting to be free too." Thinks I to myself, indeed I shall. But if he had asked me if I wanted to be free, I should have answered, "No, sir."

Of course, no slave would dare to say, in the presence of a white man, that he wished for freedom. But among themselves, it is their constant theme. No slaves think they were made to be slaves. Let them be kept ever so ignorant, it is impossible to beat it into them that they were made to be slaves. I have heard some of the most ignorant I ever saw, say, "It will not always be so, God *will* bring them to an account." I used to wonder why it was that our people were kept in slavery. I would look at the birds as they flew over my head or sung their free songs upon the trees, and think it strange, that, of all God's creatures, the poor Negro only was held in bondage. I knew there were free states, but I thought the people there did not know how we were treated. I had heard of England, and that *there*, there were no slaves; and I thought if I could only get there and tell my story, there would immediately be something done which would bring freedom to the slave.

The slaves, although kept in the lowest ignorance in which it is possible to keep them, are, nevertheless, far more intelligent than they are usually represented, or than they ever appear to white people. The few faculties they are allowed to cultivate are continually exercised, and therefore greatly strengthened; for instance, that of providing comforts for themselves and those they love, by extra work, and little trade. Then they are generally brought together from distant places and communicate to each other all the knowledge they possess. The slaves also from neighboring plantations hold frequent intercourse with each other, and then they cannot help hearing white people talk. For instance, just before the last presidential election, there came a report from a neighboring plantation, that, if Van Buren was elected, he was going to give all the slaves their freedom. It spread rapidly among all the slaves in the neighborhood, and great, very great was the rejoicing. One old man, who was a Christian, came and told us, that now, all we had got to do, was, as Moses commanded the children of Israel on the shore of the Red Sea, to "Stand still and see the salvation of God." Mr. Van Buren was elected, but he gave no freedom to the slaves.

My master was not a cruel master, only at times. He was considered a good man among slave-holders. But he was a narrow-minded, covetous, unfeeling man. His own house bore witness to his parsimony. Indeed, you would be astonished to go into many of the slave-holders' houses in that part of the country. You would know by looking into them that their hearts were not liberal enough to feed their slaves. Why, the poorest people here in New England, into whose houses I have been, have more furniture than my master's house contained, and yet he was supposed to be worth about fifty thousand dollars.

His slaves suffered more from his covetous, avaricious disposition, than from cruel punishment. His son one time gave two little pigs to my mother, which were so sickly that he despaired of raising them. They ran about the kitchen yard, and she fed them with the slops which would otherwise have been thrown away, until they got to be nice large hogs. Then my master had them put into his pen, and fatted for his own use. A deaf and dumb miller, who ground my master's wheat, gave me one time when I went to the mill, two nice little pigs, which I fatted on the produce of my little patch of ground. When they were ready, I killed one of them, and presented my master with a nice piece for his family. In a few days, he ordered me to kill the other and salt it down in his barrel. I did so, but cut out a small piece for my own use, not privately for I considered it mine, and carried it to our cabin, where we cooked and ate it at night. The next day, my master gave me a whipping for doing it, and my mother for allowing me to do it. I afterwards bought one, and was fattening it for sale, when, one time, when I was not present, he ordered it put into his pen. When I was told of it, I resolved that I would take the worth of it from him; but my mother had taught me not to steal, and I never could bring my mind to fulfil my resolution.

Such things as these we constantly suffered, and yet many of the slaves in the neighborhood would have rejoiced to belong to him, but for the circumstances that he was a regular slave-trader, making it a business to buy up slaves, and drive them away to the South; and they would be in constant fear of being sold. Yet, although he seldom whipped his slaves cruelly, at times, when he began to whip a slave, it seemed as though he never knew when to stop. He usually was drunk as often as once a week, and then, if anything occurred to enrage him, there was no limit to his fury.

One time, a slave, about forty years old, had bought some wheat of one of the neighbor's boys, which he had stolen from his master.

My master's son-in-law, Lewis Morgan, had told this slave, that, if he would buy all the wheat he could of the neighbors' slaves, he would take it of him and give him a profit. One overseer detected him with it on the way to Lewis Morgan's, and he confessed how he came by it. The overseer then took him to the master, and they went with him to the plantation where the wheat belonged, and as they passed through the field, where we were at work, they took me and another slave along with them. The thief was called up, and they were both, thief and buyer, taken to the woods, where they were stripped and tied each to a fallen tree, extended upon it face downward, with their feet and hands tied under it. The two masters commenced beating them at eight o'clock in the morning, the overseer relieving either when he was tired. They beat them with willow sticks, from five to six feet in length, tied together in bunches of from three to five, according to their size, and they continued beating them until one o'clock in the afternoon, having a bottle of rum and a pail of water standing by to drink from. Their passions seemed to rise and fall like the waves of the sea, and the poor creatures suffered accordingly.

My master whipped at this time by far the most cruelly. He would require the poor slave to confess the truth, and then to deny it, and then back again, and so on, beating him from truth to lie, and from a lie to the truth, over and over again. Of course, the slave did not tell, except to his fellow sufferers, that Lewis Morgan was concerned in the transaction, as this would only have increased his punishment. His flesh, at length, would draw and quiver all over his body, like newly killed beef, and finally it appeared as though it was dead. The poor creature was all the time shrieking, and begging, and pleading for mercy; but it had no more effect upon his torturers than would the squealing of a hog they had been killing. At one o'clock, they were released, but my poor fellow-slave was confined to his cabin two weeks before his terrible wounds were healed sufficiently for him to return to his labor. And during most of that time, whenever he was moved, you might hear him scream at a great distance.

My master, as soon as this unmerciful torture was completed, went directly to the tavern, where he had a drove of slaves ready to start, and set off for Alabama. I wish some of your people could see a drove of men, women, and children driven away to the South.

Husbands and wives, parents and children torn from each other. O! the weeping, the most dreadful weeping and howling! And it has no effect at all upon the hearts of the oppressors. They will only curse them, and whip them to make them still. When thus driven away, chained together in pairs, no attention is paid to the decency of their appearance. They go bare-headed and bare-footed, with any rag they can themselves find wrapped around their bodies. But the driver has clothing prepared for them to put on, just before they reach the market, and they are forced to array themselves with studied nicety for their exposure at public sale.

I could relate many instances of extreme cruelty practised upon plantations in our neighborhood, instances of *woman* laying heavy stripes upon the back of *woman* even under circumstances which should have removed every feeling but that of sympathy from the heart of *woman*, and which was sometimes attended with effects most shocking; of men stripped, and their flesh most terribly lacerated by the loaded whip, the sound of which might be heard on a still evening, as it fell on the naked back of the sufferer, at a great distance; of age and disease put out of the way by avarice and cruelty; but as I was not an eyewitness, and only knew them from the relations of those who did witness them, although I have myself no doubt of their truth, I forbear; assuring all, however, who may read this narrative, that *there is no sin which man can commit, that those slave-holders are not guilty of.*

One circumstance I may relate, which was so publicly known that nobody would think of disputing it, as it proves how entirely devoid of sympathy is the mind of a slave-holder with the victims of his cupidity and avarice. A slave in our neighborhood, who was a pious man, was, for some offence, threatened with whipping by his overseer. He refused to submit, and the overseer went after the master to assist him. The slave ran for the woods. The master and the overseer immediately followed and set the hounds after him. They ran him until he got to the mill-pond, into a bend of which they drove him, where there was no turning to the right or left. He had never swum, but the hounds were behind him, and he plunged in, swam to the middle of the pond, and sank to rise no more. A fellow slave, on hearing of it, went and inquired where he sank, and swam in, and diving to the bottom, he found him, took hold of his clothes with his teeth, and brought him to the shore, and he and his companions buried him. The master told them that he would give any slave a hundred lashes, who should be known to shed a tear, and several of them were whipped cruelly for this tribute of sorrow over their released fellow-sufferer. This master was the same Thomas Maguhee whom I have mentioned before.

I have been told that Paul Cameron, son of Judge Cameron, who owned a plantation out of the town where he lived, used to go out once in two or three weeks, and while there, have one or two slaves tied and whip them unmercifully, for no offence, but merely, as he said, *to let them know he was their master.*

But, to return to myself. When in my twentieth year, I became attached to a free colored girl, who lived about two miles from our plantation. When I asked my master's consent to our marriage, he refused to give it, and swore that he would cut my throat from ear to ear, before I should marry a free nigger; and with this he left me. I did not expect him to consent, but I had determined to do in this as I pleased; I knew he would not kill me, because I was money to him, and all the time keeping freedom in my view, I knew I could run away if he punished me. And so we were married. We did not dare to have any even of the trifling ceremony allowed to the slaves, but God married us.

It was about two months before my master said anything to me about it. He then attacked me one Sabbath morning, and told me I had broken his orders. He said I should not have my free wife, for he would separate us, as far as there was land to carry me. I told him if I was separated from her, I should choose to be sent away. He then told me that she was a bad girl, and endeavored by his falsehoods to make me believe it. My indignation was roused, I forgot whom I was talking to, and was on the point of giving him the lie, when I recollected myself and smothered my feelings. He then again said he would cut my throat from ear to ear, and if he had his penknife, he would do it now. I told him he might kill me if he chose, I had rather die than be separated from my wife. A man with whom he had been negotiating for overseer, was standing by, and he said to my master, "I would not do that; you know what the Scripture says about separating man and wife"; and he soon desisted and never said any more about it.

But notwithstanding my union with the object of my affection, and the comparatively good treatment I received, I still cherished the longing for liberty, which, from my childhood, had been the prevailing desire of my heart. Hitherto, my attachment to my relations, to my mother in particular, had determined me to remain as long as a strict performance of my allotted labors saved me from being whipped; but the time came, when, having obtained a knowledge of the course which would carry me to Pennsylvania, I only waited for an occasion to escape. It is very common for slaves, when whipped or threatened with a whipping, to run into the woods, and after a short time, when subdued by hunger, not knowing whither to flee for relief, to return and throw themselves upon the mercy of their masters. Therefore, when a slave runs away, on such an occasion, it is expected that he will soon return, and little trouble is taken about it for some days. For such an occasion I now waited, and it was not long before it came without my seeking it.

In May, 1837, just after I was twenty-two years old, the overseer sent a boy to me one evening, with a horse, bidding me go with him to feed him. It was then between nine and ten o'clock at night. I had toiled through the day for my master, had just got my dinner, and was on my way to the hatter's shop for my night's work, when the boy came to me. I did not think it necessary for me to go with him, so I told him where to put the horse, and that the feed was all ready and he might throw it in; and then I went to my work at the shop, where I was allowed to make hats, using nothing of my master's, except tools, and the dye which would be thrown away after my uncle had done with it.

In a few minutes, the overseer came in and asked me why I had not gone with the boy. I began to reply, by telling him that I thought he did not care if the horse was but fed, and the boy could just as well do it alone. He said he would let me know that I should obey orders, and if I did not move and feed the horse, he would thrash me as long as he could find me. I went to the house to obey him, and he followed me; but the horse was fed when I got there. He then swore that he would flog me because I had not obeyed his orders. He took a hickory rod and struck me some thirty or forty strokes, over my clothes. My first impulse was to take the stick out of his hand, for I was much stronger than he. But I recollected that my master was in the house, and if I did so, he would be called, and probably I should be stripped and tied, and instead of thirty or forty, should receive hundreds of stripes. I therefore concluded it was wisest to take quietly whatever he might choose to inflict, but as the strokes fell upon my back, I firmly resolved that I would no longer be a slave. I would now escape or die in the attempt. They might shoot me down if they chose, but I would not live a slave.

The next morning, I decided, that, as my master was preparing for one of his slave-driving expeditions to Alabama, I would wait until he was gone; that when he was fairly started on his journey, I would start on mine, he for the South, and I for the North. In the meantime, I instructed my two younger brothers in my plans. It happened that on the afternoon of the fourteenth of June, about three weeks after the whipping I received, and just after my master had set off for Alabama, as we were going to the field after breakfast, to ploughing, the overseer got very angry with me and my two brothers, and threatened to whip us before night. He said that as he could not do it himself, there were men in the neighborhood he could get to help him, and then he walked away. This was our opportunity. We took our horses round to the road fence and hitched them, and ran for my wife's house. There I changed my clothes, and took my leave of her, with the hope of being soon able to send for her from a land of freedom, and left her in a state of distress which I cannot describe.

We started without money and without clothes, except what we wore, not daring to carry a bundle, but with our hearts full of hope. We travelled by night, and slept in the woods during the day. After travelling two or three nights, we got alarmed and turned out of the road, and before we turned into it again, it had separated, and we took the wrong road. It was cloudy for two or three days, and, after travelling three nights, we found ourselves just where we were three days before, and almost home again. We were sadly disappointed, but not discouraged; and so, turning our faces again northward, we went on.

I should have said before, that I knew the way to Petersburg, Virginia, having been several times sent there by my master with a team. Near Petersburg, we passed a neat farmhouse, with everything around it in perfect order, which had once been shown to me by a slave, as I was driving my master's team to the city. "That," said he, "belongs to a Friend; they never hold slaves." Now I was strongly tempted to stop there, and ask instructions in my northward course, as I knew the way no farther; but I dared not. So, not knowing the North Star, we took the lower star of the Great Bear for our guide, and putting our trust in God, we passed Petersburg.

We suffered much from hunger. There was no fruit and no grain to be found at that season, and we sometimes went two days, and sometimes three, without tasting food, as we did not dare to ask, except when we found a slave's, or free colored person's house remote from any other, and then we were never refused, if they had food to give. Thus we came on, until about forty-five miles from Washington, when, having in the night obtained some meal, and having then been three days without food, my poor brothers begged me to go out of the woods in the day time, and get some fire in order to bake us some bread. I went to a house, got some and returned to the woods. We made a fire in the hollow stump of a tree, mixed our meal with water, which we found near, and wrapping it in leaves, threw it in and baked it.

After eating heartily, we began to bake some to carry with us, when hearing a noise in the bushes, we looked up, and beheld dogs coming towards us, and behind them several white men, who called out, "O! You rascals, what are you doing there? Catch him! Catch him!" The dogs sprang towards us. My feelings I cannot describe, as I started, and ran with all my might. My brothers, having taken off their coats and hats, stopped to pick them up, and then ran off in another direction, and the dogs followed them, while I escaped and never saw them more. I heard the dogs barking after them, when I had got as much as a mile from where we started.

O! then I was most miserable, left alone, a poor hunted stranger in a strange land—my brothers gone. I know not how to express the feelings of that moment. After listening awhile, I went forward. I had lost my way, and knew not where I was, but I looked at the sun, and as near as I could, pursued a northward course. In that afternoon I was attacked by a wild beast. I knew not what it was. I thought, surely I am beset this day, but unlike the men, more ferocious than wild beasts, I succeeded in driving him away, and that night crossed a branch of the Potomac.

Just before I reached the town of Dumfries, I came across an old horse in a field with a bell on his neck. I had been warned by a colored man, a few nights before, to beware of Dumfries. I was worn out with running, and I took the bell off the horse's neck, took the bell collar for a whip, and putting a hickory bark round his head for a bridle, I jumped on his back, and thus mounted, I rode through Dumfries. The bulldogs lay along the street, ready to seize the poor night traveller, but being on horseback, they did not molest me. I have no doubt that I should have been taken up, if I had been on foot. When I got through the town, I dismounted, and said to my horse, "Go back to your master, I did not mean to injure him, and hope he will get you again, but you have done me a great deal of good." And then I hastened on, and got as far from him as I could before morning.

At Alexandria, I crossed the Potomac river, and came to Washington, where I made friends with a colored family, with whom I rested eight days. I then took the Montgomery road, but, wishing to escape Baltimore, I turned off, and it being cloudy, I lost my course, and fell back again upon the Potomac river, and travelled on the tow-path of the canal from Friday night until Sunday morning, when I lay down and slept a little, and then, having no place to hide for the day, I determined to go on until I could find a place of safety.

I soon saw a man riding towards me on horseback. As he came near, he put his eyes upon me, and I felt sure that he intended to question me. I fell to praying to God to protect me, and so begging and praying fervently, I went forward. When he met me, he stopped his horse, leaned forward, and looked at me, and then, without speaking, rode on again. I still fully believe it was at first his intention to question me. I soon entered a colored person's house on the side of the canal, where they gave me breakfast and treated me very kindly. I travelled on through Williamsport and Hagerstown, in Maryland, and, on the nineteenth day of July, about two hours before day, I crossed the line into Pennsylvania, with a heart full of gratitude to God, believing that I was indeed a free man, and that now, under the protection of law, there was "None who could molest me or make me afraid."

In the course of the morning, I was spoken to by a man, sitting at the window of a house in Chambersburg, who asked me if I wanted a job of work. I replied that I did, and he took me into his garden, and set me to work. When the job was done, he told me I might clean his carriage. At dinner, I ate in the kitchen with a colored woman. She inquired where I came from. I told her the name of a town in Pennsylvania. Said she, "I didn't know but you come from Virginia, or Maryland, and sometimes, some of our colored friends come from there hither, and think they are free, but the people about here are very ugly, and they take them and carry them back; and if you haven't sufficient free papers, I would advise you not to stay here tonight.

This was enough for me. I had discovered that the man was very curious about me, and seemed disposed to keep me at work upon little jobs until night. I went out, and jumped over the garden wall, and was soon on the turnpike road. I was very fearful, and came on tremblingly; but near Philadelphia, I fell in with members of the Society of Friends, whom I never feared to trust, and I worked for them until Christmas.

After finding, to my great disappointment, that I was not a free man and that I could not send for my wife from here, I determined to go to Canada. But the situation of that country at that time was such that my friends thought it was not best for me to go immediately, and advised me to come into the state of Massachusetts, as the safest place for me until the difficulties in Canada had passed away. I was taken by kind Friends to New York, from whence the Abolitionists sent me to Fall River, Massachusetts, and here I have found a resting place, and have met with friends who have freely administered to my necessities, and whose kindness to the poor fugitive I shall ever remember with emotions of heartfelt gratitude.

Letters to Family, Friends and the *Providence Journal*

by Elizabeth Buffum Chace,

1854–1898

Mrs. Chace to Samuel Chace

Valley Falls, 4th mo., 3rd, 1854. Yesterday I promised Eddie that I would buy a stick of molasses candy for him, but I forgot it until after supper tonight and then gave Lillie three cents to go and buy some. She wished Arnold to go with her. When they returned, she brought four sticks and, according to my promise, I gave Eddie one. I then broke one in two and gave it to Arnold, bidding him give one half to Sammy. He said he wanted a whole stick, and kept on fretting and scolding. Finally he threw the half stick in my lap and said he would not have it. I said he should not and arose with it. He screamed and endeavored to force it from me and finding he could not, he commenced striking me. I seized his hands and held them and bade Mary help me to undress him, but he kicked so we could not and I sent out after Michael; I holding his hands the meanwhile and he kicking and pulling in the most violent anger. Michael came and all three of us with the utmost difficulty divested him of his clothing, put on his nightgown, and then Michael laid him in bed. All this time I felt perfectly calm, without the slightest irritation. Something whispered encouragement in my spirit, saying, "Do it thoroughly; it will be the last time." At first I told Michael to sit down by the bedside, for I feared he would attempt to get out the window; but I soon saw he had no idea of doing that, and so I sent Michael out. Arnold opened the door into the bathroom and I let it remain so. He took all his bedclothes and strewed them on the floor; pulled off the mattresses; pulled out the bed cord and then went to the bookcase which stood in the room and took out every book and paper and threw it on the floor. The other children had gone to bed and nobody interfered with him. Then his angry passion seemed to have spent itself. He lay down and wept. It grew pretty dark and he was alone. After a while he came out sobbing and said, "Mother, will thee get me a little stick to put the strings into my bedstead?" (meaning the bed cord. The bedstead has holes for the cord to go through). I gave him a fork and he went back. Sammy volunteered his assistance and by the dim twilight they put in the cord and put on the beds and then Sammy left him and he made up the bed. Then he went to the bookcase and commenced putting up the books and papers, in the dark. I let him work a while and then set a light in the room and he returned them all nicely to their places. Then he brought out the light, bade me farewell, and went to bed. I hoped he would come and acknowledge his fault, but did not think it best to draw this from him but to leave him entirely to his own thoughts. It was a crisis to which he had been for some time tending and I think it will do him good.

Should this record meet his eye in the future years, I doubt not that he will gratefully acknowledge that his mother did him no injustice and that her firmness helped him to overcome his obstinacy.

Mrs. Chace to Effingham L. Capron

Valley Falls, 2nd mo., 1858. It has been so much my fortune to hold unusual opinions, thereby rendering myself a sort of outlaw, that I feel very cautious how I venture to raise an issue between myself and the beloved few, who have hitherto sympathized with and encouraged me.

For a long time I could not but suppose that other people when so informed would, like me, see only the path of ceasing to do wrong. In this I was disappointed. Most people had so many things to take into consideration, so many prejudices and fears to listen to before they could decide that it was safe to do right, that, after years of effort, I have been for a long time endeavoring to reconcile right with wrong, have, by an inevitable law in morals, lost the power to discriminate between the two. Still, the truth and the right are not lost, and a crisis is approaching in which, after conflict, by another Divine law, the right will prevail and justice will be done. Whether this conflict shall be a peaceful one depends upon the influential to decide.

My dear friend, I feel very much indebted to thee for the strong impulse which thy kindness and good taste gave, in my early youth, to my love for literature, a love which I have always found means to gratify; and it would be cause of great satisfaction to me, if I could repay thee therefore, by assisting thee in one step towards the advocacy of right on high moral ground, regardless of consequences; for there *are* no consequences worthy to be thought of in deciding whether we will do right or wrong.

I have learned to believe, that there can be but *one true* marriage, for any human soul, and that this is to be eternal; and it seems to me, that, when this has been attained on earth, to a certainty of conviction, there should, naturally, be no desire for a union with another. But this true union does not take place, in nine cases out of ten, and in such circumstances, the unsatisfied soul would, in case of separation by death, continue to seek its mate, and it seems perfectly natural and right, that trial after trial should thus be made.

Mrs. Chace to Arnold B. Chace

Home, 19th, 2nd mo., 1860. I think I never received a letter which gave me more satisfaction than thine of the 12th inst., because of the evidence it contained that thou wert seeking to know the Truth, and wishing to [do] the Right.

I will try to answer thy question in regard to principles and prayer, according to the best light which my experience, my reason and my impressions have given me.

All truth, all goodness, all principles come from God. Error and evil arise from ignorance, and the disorder resulting from ignorance, or misunderstanding of what is for our true interest and happiness.

In the midst of all this, the Spirit of God is ever seeking, through various instrumentalities, to restore order among mankind, to elevate, purify and educate men, [so that] they shall in all circumstances endeavor to learn what is right, and then do it, at whatever cost, *because it is right*. Now, whenever any person is seeking to bring *himself* into this state, he is acting in harmony with God; is cooperating with Him in His great design, is becoming one of the instruments in the Divine economy for the accomplishment of this work. Every desire that animates him in his effort is accompanied by a consciousness that it is in accordance with the Divine will, and thus he is brought into communion with God. A person in this state will often turn his thoughts upward, in order to gain new strength for future and greater efforts in behalf of the right, and for help to overcome, in his heart and his life, all that retards his progress towards a higher and better state. And *this is true prayer*, whether it is framed in words or not.

Also, a person will, in moments of reflection, feel the need of more strength to resist temptation, than he finds within himself. He may (and I think it is very natural that he should) in earnest words implore his Heavenly Father to help him to keep his good resolutions, and the desires which prompt these words will carry him beneath the very arms of Divine protection. For God is always extending toward us a helping hand. *If we reach out for it*, it helps us; and this reaching out is prayer.

Also, when we are anxiously concerned for the welfare of others, we are especially in harmony with God; and, while doing all we can to aid them, we are very naturally led to ask of Him to throw around them such influences as will lead them aright. Not doubting that He is ever watching over them, either directly or through the agency of spirits, yet, we seem so naturally led to request His care over them, that I always feel as though, in some way which we yet do not quite understand, such prayers have some influence for good upon them.

And upon ourselves, I know that, like everything we do for others, the effect is always beneficial.

All this is quite a different thing, as thou, my dear child, wilt readily perceive, from any formal ceremony of saying words in a solemn tone to God, as a religious rite, of going somewhere, at stated seasons, to perform a prayer, and then feeling that so much work is done;—one person usually performing for a whole congregation.

No prayer is *mine* unless it goes from my heart, or finds a response therein; and whatever does, is good for me, in whatever way the Divine Providence may answer it.

I trust what I have written will be enough for the present. It has given me great pleasure to write it, and I think some benefit, and I hope that thou wilt receive both in reading it, both thou and dear Sammie, for whose welfare and progress in all that is good, many an earnest prayer ascends from your mother's heart.

I like the house [the Homestead] better and better all the time; it seems more like home than the other did. Last night, we all slept upstairs, and I had very little, if any, of the fear I used to have so much of at the other house, when your father was gone. Still, I thought it would have been nice to have had you at home.

I see by the *Liberator* that Garrison was to speak today at Milford. If you heard him, you must tell me about it. This week Frederick Brown, brother of the martyr, is to speak at Pawtucket. I hope to hear him.

The temperance meetings are continued here, and are very largely attended. I think they are doing a good work. But there is much to do to civilize and elevate the people. I hope when you get to be men, you will be fitted to do some of it, by having elevated and purified yourselves. Give Sammie much love from thine and his loving mother.

Mrs. Chace to Lucy F. Lovell

Valley Falls, Aug. 13th, 1861. Mr. Garrison and his wife came Thursday night and in the morning Mr. Garrison went into Providence and returned bringing with him his only daughter, Miss Helen Frances Garrison—called Fanny, a pretty, bright girl of sixteen, overflowing with fun—in that respect resembling her respected "pater" as she termed him, only of course her fun is of a younger and more girlish sort.

Saturday morning we were going huckleberrying, Mr. Garrison with us. Only think of it, going huckleberrying with a man whose name shall live fresh and green when the Napoleons are forgotten. But alas, we were destined to be disappointed; the morning was cloudy and threatened rain. Fanny and I substituted a walk with Mr. Garrison and Arnold.

Sunday evening we had company to hear the great Abolitionist converse. A part of the evening we were in the library, cutting up, leaving the sober old folks to the quiet possession of the parlor, but finally we adjourned to the parlor, and heard Garrison, and any one else who chose to talk. I had the pleasure of hearing my handsome, last year married, cousin James talk real good anti-slavery, part of which may be owing to his subscribing to the *Liberator* the day he was married, Lucretia having said she would like it.

Monday we went huckleberrying without Mr. Garrison, because he and his wife and daughter thought he would get all tired and burnt. His wife said he always burnt his nose and looked like an old toper. We—six of us—got twenty-eight quarts, and on our return were greeted by all in the vestibule, Mr. Garrison, according to his habit, waving his hat to us, and Fanny, in pulling off hers to respond, pulled off her net, and down streamed her hair, nearly to her waist, so we entered the yard with screams of laughter.

Aug. 14th, 1861. In regard to President Lincoln,—does thou not see that however good may be his desires, he can do very little towards setting things right? Surrounded as he must be by ambitious, intriguing men, who are only bent on the advancement of their own interests, he can be little else than a tool in their hands. Oh! no; for the removal of the great wrong which we have set up in the place of all that is called God, until the nation has become corrupt,—it is useless to look for reform from politicians or government. It can only come through the awakening of the consciences of the people, and the inevitable march of those immutable laws by which finally,

> Ever the right comes uppermost,
> And ever is justice done.

Mrs. Chace to Lillie Buffum Chace

Valley Falls, 10th, 17th, 1865. About thy going to Roxbury and Milton. Thee says thee thinks of spending next Sunday at Roxbury; then thee speaks of thy letter from Mr. Mumford, and says thee thinks thee shall accept his invitation which is for the same day. It makes me very uneasy. I cannot have thee going from one town to another alone, with nobody to know whether thee gets there or not and back again. So let me say if thee wants to go to Roxbury next Seventh Day, either go with Mr. Weld, and be left by daylight near Mr. Garrison's; or else go to Boston with Eddie and let him put thee, in the daytime, on the cars which will take thee to Roxbury, and then stay there till thee comes back [to Lexington], or else if thee goes to Milton get Fanny or somebody to go with thee or take Eddie with thee.

Mrs. Chace to Arnold B. Chace

Basle, 9th mo., 2nd, 1872.

My dear fatherly boy:—

We arrived here yesterday and found thy letters announcing the arrival of the grandbaby. Mary is quite displeased because he presumed to be a boy. Lillie is at this moment embroidering his afghan blanket and I am trying to realize the wondrous fact that I am a grandmother! I hope he will live and grow finely until we get home.

I want to see him amazingly. Keep him warm, and carry him outdoors every day when it is pleasant.

Mrs. Chace to Gov. Henry Lippitt

Valley Falls, 12th mo., 31st, 1876. Your letter of inquiry is received, and I thank you for the interest it manifests in an important question.

My conviction that women should have an equal share with men in the management of all penal and reformatory institutions not only remains unchanged, but is continually confirmed and strengthened by actual experience.

In the case of the female inmates, only women can fully understand their peculiar characteristics and necessities; and women only can thoroughly investigate their actual condition and the treatment they receive at the hands of those employed in their immediate control.

In the treatment of male criminals, the influence of women is also of great usefulness; and will often accomplish more for their discipline and benefit than could possibly be effected by the efforts of men alone. The motherly voice of a kind, judicious woman will sometimes reach the hardened conscience, when that of a man, equally wise and kind, might appeal to it in vain. My judgment therefore is, that the boards of direction and control of all these institutions should be composed of both men and women, endowed alike with power.

There cannot be two bodies, one of men and the other of women, having an equal voice in the management of the same institution. And where one is vested with power and the other is not, it is vain to expect harmonious or useful coöperation to any very valuable extent.

In the counsels of a board of men and women, the aid of the women would be found to be invaluable, from their keen insight into character, their clear moral perceptions, and their large experience in all household arrangements.

It is therefore my settled conviction and earnest wish, that our Legislature, at its next session, should make some provision whereby women shall be appointed on each one of the following boards: State Charities and Corrections, Inspectors of the State Prison, and Trustees of the Reform School.

I cannot immediately say what is the number of our female prisoners; but it is usually less than one-third that of the male.

Will you allow me to suggest that you do also recommend to the legislature the establishment of an industrial school for the prevention of juvenile criminality.

Mrs. Chace to Mrs. Elizabeth K. Churchill

4th mo., 13th, 1877. I cannot acknowledge that I have "cast off" any of my friends "because they do not view any question from my precise point." I certainly have always known that thee and I differed widely in our opinions concerning theology, and

Christianity, and all matters pertaining to religion. Still, this has not separated us.

But, when thee says, "if you require agreement upon all points that you deem vital and involving principle, your friends must be few," if thee means moral principle, it is in a measure true, so far as close, intimate friendship is concerned.

Of course, I can be friendly, and often am, toward persons who seem to me defective in, or even destitute of, moral principle, but I cannot take them to my heart, and feel or act towards them as I do towards persons whom I love because their ideas of right and wrong are true and just, and their actions are in accordance therewith.

In the Woman's Club, Mrs. Palmer declares, as I am told, that with her, it is a principle, that people of different races should not mingle together. If she is sincere in believing so, and acts conscientiously, although I consider her mistaken, I respect her for standing by her beliefs, until she learns that it is a prejudice born of the oppression of one race by another, which has produced its legitimate result of hatred of the oppressed by the oppressor. If she is honest, I have no doubt but the example and arguments of those who see more clearly, will, in time, lead her to see the injustice of her position towards the colored people of this country.

Mrs. Chace to the *Providence Journal* (Extracts)

I have waited from day to day, hoping that some one would express, through the *Journal*, the moral sentiment of Rhode Island concerning the pigeon shooting at Newport, of which such a detailed report appeared in a late number of your paper.

When factory boys are arrested for cock-fighting, and subjected to fine and imprisonment, through the agency of the "Society for the Prevention of Cruelty to Animals," how will the difference be explained to them between their cruel crime and the fine affair at Newport, which results in the torture of pigeons by the fashionable and wealthy actors? Do not both the cock-fighting and the pigeon-shooting have their origin in the same brutal instincts as the bull-fights of Spain and the gladiatorial combats of ancient Rome? And shall Rhode Island civilization do honor to such scenes?

Extracts from an Article on the Prevention of Pauperism and Crime, by Mrs. Chace, printed in the *Providence Journal*, August 27, 1877

The tendency to pauperism and crime has so alarmingly increased in this country, that it is become a positive necessity for the safety of the state that some improved methods should be adopted for its prevention and cure.

I propose to discuss only the best means of saving the children who have lately come into existence under circumstances most unfavorable to the development of good character.

Of course, there is no place in the world so excellent for training as a good home, but when parents become a burden or a danger to the state, then the commonwealth owes to its own safety, and to the children, such provisions as shall preserve them, if possible, from following in the parental footsteps.

Our state has never yet made any special provision for the children of drunkards and criminals when the parents are condemned to imprisonment.

Let us build a home for such children, and let this home be so situated and so managed that it shall entirely remove its inmates from all degrading and disreputable circumstances; and let us adopt therein every possible method to train them into good citizenship.

That the life in it may be as much as possible like family life, I would have it built in this wise. There should be a large, plain, central building, in which should be kitchen, laundry, dining room, school rooms, workshop, hall and sleeping rooms for adult persons employed therein. Then the plan should be to build a circle of cottages around the central house, all facing toward it, with plenty of space between them for free circulation of air, and also between them and the central building for a large playground and avenues. It would be necessary to begin with only one or two cottages. In each cottage I would place a good woman and a certain number of children; and this should be their home. The whole establishment and head matron, who should also live in a cottage in the circle in order to have the whole institution under their eyes.

I would have the boys and girls in this institution so guarded and trained that they should learn to behave properly in the presence of each other, as children do in families; always being taught that what is wrong in one sex is equally wrong in the other.

I would have the state searched for the best and wisest men and women to constitute a board of control for this institution. They should be persons of large experience and yet of such leisure as to be able to devote much time to this work.

These persons should have no connection with penal or pauper institutions because every effort should be made to keep this school distinct from such places.

Indeed the education should be such as to make it a recommendation for any person seeking a situation, in any business for which he is qualified, that he is a graduate of this school.

I am fully aware that an institution such as I advocate would involve great expense. But I have much faith that a few years would prove it a great economy. Indeed, I foresee that the additions and extensions of our prisons and alms houses which we are constantly taxed to supply, might soon cease altogether and in time, perhaps, these places themselves be nearly superseded by "this wisest of our state charities."

Mrs. Chace to Miss Sarah E. Doyle

Valley Falls, 6th mo., 4th, 1878. I thank you for the courtesy of your note. I shall be very happy to do anything I can, when the time comes, for the entertainment of the A.A.W., and I know now to prevent me from inviting some of its members from abroad to the hospitality of my house. But I cannot accept your invitation for tomorrow evening. The attitude of the R.I. Woman's Club toward the colored women of Rhode Island and its treatment of its dissenting members preclude all possibility of my cooperation or fellowship with it.

My "interest in all subjects relating to women" is not limited by the color of their skin, but includes all women, and is given most to those who need it most.

The reading of an essay, by a colored woman, on the Colored Women of America, before the Woman's Congress in 1876, has deepened my interest in the A.A.W., and, as I said before, I will do all I can to give it welcome and support in Providence.

Mrs. Chace to the *Providence Journal* (Extracts)

Jan. 20, 1879. The friends with whom I am visiting and myself have been twice to hear Prof. Felix Adler, who lectures every Sunday morning in Standard Hall, before the "Society for Ethical Culture." He is, as is well known, the son of a Jewish rabbi in this city, has been a professor in Cornell University, but is now living here, and devoting himself to humanitarian work. This winter, he is delivering a series of lectures on "the duties of life," in which he advocates, as the essence of true religion, the highest morality, truthfulness, integrity, absolute purity of heart and life, holding men amenable to the same law that governs women.

Mr. Adler does not condemn the individual accumulation of property, but [he says] the motive should be, not that the possessor may be enriched for his own aggrandizement, but that his power of doing good to those less endowed may be enlarged. When we give money to those who render us service, as the physician, the lawyer, the minister, etc., the motive should be, not to pay them for their work, which should be unselfishly performed, but to sustain them in the performance of still greater service to mankind.

The following evening, we attended a reception given in private parlors to Sojourner Truth, the distinguished woman, once a slave in New York, emancipated by the act which, in the year 1817, set free all the slaves in this state over forty years of age. She is therefore at least one hundred and five years old. She received the guests sitting, having been partially paralyzed, but she looked in good health, and her remembrance of friends whom she had not met for years is remarkable. Clad in a neat, plain garb, her bright, intelligent face beaming out from beneath a Quaker-like cap, she looked the prophetess and seer she has many years been, in the ranks of reform. When, after many congratulations followed by music and singing, she stood up and addressed the audience for nearly an hour, though the originality and brilliancy, in her utterances of many years ago, were quite diminished, yet her spirit, if less fiery, was lofty and uplifting, and her repetition of some of her old sayings was strikingly effective. One which I remember having heard long ago from her lips was especially inspiring to me at this time. In answer to some one who questioned whether she believed in the everlasting existence of evil and its punishment, she replied: "Of course not. Everything that had a beginning must come to an end. Goodness existed always, and therefore will be eternal. But evil began with sin and sin must come to an end." At a late hour we left her, still standing, her tall form erect and steady, her voice clear and strong, declaring her undying and unfaltering faith in the power and the eternity of goodness.

Another evening we attended a meeting of the "Committee to Prevent the State Regulation of Vice," a measure which has been recommended in New York by one, at least, of its eminent physicians; and, what is stranger still, by the Board of Charities and Corrections.

Mrs. Chace to the *Providence Journal* (Extracts)

Feb. 10, 1879. "The Isaac T. Hopper Home" had a special interest for me, because I have long desired that we might have, in our own city, a place of refuge and reform for the homeless, friendless, sorely tempted women, who are discharged, unreformed, from our penal institutions. I therefore gladly accepted the invitation of one of its managers, to accompany her on a morning visit. This home was established many years ago, through the efforts of the philanthropist whose name it bears, and is under the management of the Woman's Prison Association, of which Abby Hopper Gibbons, daughter of its founder, is the president.

Women discharged from prison are invited to enter it [this home] on condition that they will work for its interest for one month, and they are there fed, clothed and furnished with employment. At the expiration of that time they are permitted to go out to service, making a home elsewhere, or they go out to work by the day and return for lodging at night, paying a small fee for whatever they require. If, on going out, a woman returns drunk, she is not received, but sent to the station house, although Mrs. Gibbons told me they overlook, as much as possible, slight offenses of this kind, and try to keep a hold upon the woman as long as they can.

I was very glad of my visit to the Tombs, because its name and all I had ever heard had given me a gloomy picture of this place of detention; but I found it better than I expected. It is dark and dismal and damp, but it is kept very clean and as dry as good fires can make it. Lime is used very freely, even the floors being whitewashed.

As we passed the door of the cells in the doors of the cells in the men's department and looked in on their anxious faces, I was shocked, as I always am in prisons, by the large proportion of very young men, some of them almost boys, awaiting trial for murder, burglary, robbery and other heinous crimes. I spoke of this to two officers in attendance, and one of them replied: "Yes, but they are often not very bad, if they were handled rightly. It is the hard times compels them often. Going by a shop window, they are tempted to break a pane of glass and take something. They don't know the law, but it is burglary, and so they get sent up for five years."

When we know that a lonely imprisonment means in most cases a hardening of the heart and a deadening of the conscience, so that the man will be a more dangerous person when he comes out, than he was when he went in, this being "sent up for five years" has an ominous sound, which, in the case of such boys, it is not pleasant to hear.

In the woman's department the scene was sad enough. The bloated faces, the bleared and bloodshot eyes, the vacant stare of the confirmed victims of the system which makes drunkards by law, the young girls brought there *alone*, for suspicious conduct on the street, the pale, worn faces of the sorely tempted women whose self-control was insufficient to prevent the unlawful appropriation of their neighbor's goods; their tears and wails over little children left at home with no one to care for them, were heartrending. The matron of the institution is a woman who has occupied the position for thirty years; and she still has a cheerful spirit and a kind, sympathizing heart; at the same time she has a strong will and great controlling power. Her plain common sense and her sound judgment struck me forcibly. I should like to see her on the judicial bench.

From the Tombs we went into the Court of Special Sessions, which sits close by, with three judges on the bench. Here two features impressed me with sorrow and indignation. The first was, the presence of a large number of boys, who filled one-fourth of the seats for spectators, and they sat there learning lessons which in a few years will bring many of them before the bar. The other was the fact that, in a trial for assault upon a woman by a man, in which the testimony of both was heard, the treatment of the woman by a lawyer and the judges was far more harsh and offensive than that of the man. But my days were not all spent in these sorrowful scenes.

Dr. John Lord is delivering a course of lectures in Chickering Hall, and thither, one morning, I accompanied a friend to listen to one on St. Augustine.

I heard Anna Dickinson's lecture on the platform and the stage; and while I assented to much of her criticism of the platform, the pulpit and the press, I could not agree that, as a moral influence, the stage is, as she claims, superior to them all. While the manager of one of the best theatres in New York, in putting upon the stage the charming little drama of *The Cricket on the Hearth*, feels obliged to precede it by a display upon which no man or woman ought to be able to look without shame, and a sense of insult, I cannot believe the moral effect, as a whole, of the modern stage is yet of a very elevating character. I think it ought to be what Miss Dickinson claims that it is.

There is much work for humanity in progress in the great world of New York, a little of which I saw and much of which I heard. But nothing which I saw or heard gave me so much hope and courage as the kindergartens. And, coming home to Rhode Island, I could not but bring with me a strong desire that, in our own city and state, we should devise more thorough measures than we have yet tried for the saving of the children. The institution of the state school for dependent, homeless children, which some of us have so sought for, and the establishment of public kindergartens, seem to me the two instrumentalities most needed and best fitted for this purpose.

Fifteen months before her own death, that is, in the year 1898, Mrs. Chace wrote thus:

Parker Pillsbury was one of the most self-sacrificing and eloquent of the anti-slavery speakers. Once, when at my house in the autumn on his way to some other point, I asked him at what time he would give us a lecture. He said he should attend the annual meeting of the Society the next May in New York, and could come to Rhode Island on his return from that. So the day was fixed and he went away.

The winter months rolled by and the early spring, and I received no word from him. The day came on which he had promised to appear. I had engaged the hall and advertised the lecture. As the sun went down I began to feel anxious, and finally decided that it was hardly possible that he could have remembered the engagement. It grew dark, and I began to plan for announcing the failure of the meeting, when, hearing a click at the gate, I looked out and saw Parker Pillsbury walking into the yard. If he had dropped from the skies I could not have been more surprised. He was one of the never-failing kind.

· 8 ·

An Address on Women's Suffrage

by Elizabeth Buffum Chace,

Written in 1891

*I*n the early days of the settlement of Rhode Island, the women who accompanied our forefathers to these colonies, bravely shared in all the discomforts and privations incident to the building up of new homes on uncultivated ground and among an uncivilized people. Many of these settlers were refugees from the puritanic persecutions in Massachusetts, and, I presume, if the truth were known, the women rendered valuable service in devising that rare system of religious liberty and toleration by which our commonwealth has, more than any other in the world, deserved that worthy name. In the history of that time, stands out the name of one woman, the ancestor of one of Rhode Island's oldest families, whose memory her descendants now living here, may well hold in the deepest reverence. This was Mary

Dyer, wife of William Dyer, the first general recorder of the province
of Rhode Island. Directed, as she believed, by the Holy Spirit, she
went to Boston, to plead with the authorities there for mercy to the
persecuted Quakers, and was banished therefrom on pain of death.
Returning home to her family, she soon believed she heard the inner
voice bringing to her a divine summons to return to Massachusetts
on a second mission. This she heroically obeyed; and, in the year
1660, she suffered a cruel death by hanging on Boston Common.

Written history, however, except in rare instances, makes little mention of women or their deeds; but, tradition often hands down in families, the record of great nobility of character in the private womanhood
of past generations. And such records are not wanting here. When the
War of the Revolution came, Rhode Island women were found ready
to perform all the duties and to endure all the hardships of that perilous
period. In the year 1777, the island of R.I. was in possession of the
British forces. John Fiske, in his history of the American Revolution,
states that, under the rule of the commander, "no citizen of Newport
was safe in his own house. He not only arrested people and threw them
into jail without assigning any reason, but he encouraged his soldiers in
plundering houses, and offering insult to ladies." "If he chanced to
meet a Quaker who failed to take off his hat, he would seize him by the
collar, and knock his head against the wall, or strike him with the gnarled
stick he usually carried." I know of one Newport woman, whose house
was invaded at that time by British officers; they taking its best apart-
ments and its best household supplies, giving such orders as they chose
to its inmates. This woman had one daughter, a fair maiden of sixteen,
who was one of that galaxy of beauties for which our lovely island was
famous. According to the custom of the time, it was this girl's duty to
milk the family cows. That mother let her child out of a bedroom
window with milk-pails, at early morning, and again at evening, and
waited to take her in, keeping a constant watch that the eyes of no rude
Britishers might ever rest on the fair young face. Every hour of her
time, for she had many children, was filled with numerous and wearing
cares. One day a French officer was brought bleeding into the house,
from a skirmish with the British in a field near by, and placed on a bed
in an apartment usually occupied by the enemy. This woman, who did
not dare to let her husband enter their rooms, went in herself, to assist
in dressing the poor fellow's wounds. And, when the English officers
came rushing in, brandishing their swords and threatening him with

instant death, she calmly looked them in the face, and rebuked their savage instincts for the time, and, until he recovered, she continued to minister to his necessities with her own fair hands. What days and nights of anxiety, what care and trouble she endured, what fear she smothered in her own brave heart, no historian has ever chronicled. But, with other women like her, she, Quaker as she was, and hating war, did a worthy and a peaceful part, in giving us a country of our own.

Another woman, a generation earlier still, reared in the town of Smithfield, eight stalwart sons and six noble daughters, who all lived to build up households of their own; and, when her children were well-grown, she took eight friendless, destitute children, one after another, and brought them up in her own house. A granddaughter of hers, whom I knew many years ago, told me that this woman, even in her old age, was the counselor, the doctor, the nurse and lawyer among the scattered people of all the region round about her; and that no man among them would have bought or sold a farm, or entered into any new business, without consulting "Aunt Margaret," as she was uniformly called. Her descendants are to be found, at this day, in at least twelve towns in this state; and, among them have been jurists, statesmen, preachers and philanthropists, as well as farmers, merchants and manufacturers; and I have never heard of one of them being supported by any of our towns or by the state, either as a pauper or a criminal. In the long struggle for the overthrow of slavery, when to be an avowed abolitionist meant social disgrace, sectarian disapproval, and danger of mob violence, there were Rhode Island women who braved all these for the sake of the down-trodden slave.

It is too early now to write any sketch of the efforts of Rhode Island women, in the cause of temperance and the prohibition of the liquor traffic; but, in the history written in the future, when men are more just to women, it will be shown that they bore a worthy part in this great reformation.

My own recollections carry me back to a period, when the chief occupation of the citizens of Rhode Island, outside of Newport and Providence, was farming. And, all up and down these country roads lived women to whom it was no play to be prosperous farmers' wives and daughters. The flax from the time it was plucked from the ground, the wool as it was sheared from the sheep, the milk as it came from the cows, with many other products of the farm, were all consigned to the women, to be converted by their never idle hands, into clothing, food, and other comforts and luxuries for the household; the surplus frequently to be disposed of, as a means of furnishing their own wardrobes with such necessary articles as the farm did not produce. And yet, these women, many of them, were not only shrewd in matters of business, but, they were readers of books, and thinkers on all questions which were then considered to be of national, state, or town concern. They talked politics with their husbands and neighbors, and read with eagerness the current news, as it was brought weekly to their doors, by *The Manufacturers' and Farmers' Journal*, at that time, the leading authority in all matters of public interest. Of course, they were bred in the old ideas concerning women; and their duties kept them chiefly confined to their homes. A woman who was often seen abroad, was called in derision, "a spinner of street yarn." Then, we were under the old common law, as it was inherited from our English ancestry. We had not full manhood suffrage. Only men owning land could vote. The idea of women voting had not entered the Rhode Island mind. Married women had no property rights. Whatever they owned before marriage, or inherited afterward, became at once, the property of their husbands; and it was a common remark, when a rich girl married, that "she brought her husband a handsome fortune." After marriage, she was expected to "pay her way," by women in well-to-do households, and, she was considered fortunate, if her husband provided liberally for the support of the family, and especially, if he indulged her tastes in personal expenses. Her identity as a person, was entirely merged in that of her husband. "Man and wife were one," and that one was the man.

This state of the married woman was reflected upon the unmarried; and the daughters in a family were considered of far less value than the sons, because the work they did brought in no money and so, they were supposed not to earn anything; but to be only an expense to their fathers. The men, old and young, were the heads of the household. Outside of Quaker families, rich men sent their sons to college. It was not thought necessary or wise for girls to learn beyond the three R's. Brown University was established for the higher education of "the youth of the state"; but that meant only the boys. The women and girls never thought of asking for admission. They were satisfied to stay at home and work, that the boys might go. And yet, as I have said, there was much intellectual and practical ability and wisdom among them, which, combined with that of the men, in the construction and government of the state, might have made there of a place fit for gods to dwell in. But their time for protest had not come; and it would have cost a woman her reputation, to say she had not all the rights she wanted. And now, with broader opportunities, with more education and enlightenment, with modern improvements, that render house-hold labors and cares less onerous and absorbing, giving leisure to women to look about them for wider activities, in which, as they enter, women are showing remarkable ability and faithfulness, let us consider what is the legal status, what are the customs to which the daughters and successors of those earlier women are now subjected in Rhode Island. Looking over the broad ground of the world, we see every where, signs of growth toward the elevation of women—Australia taking steps for their enfranchisement, India for their education, China and Persia catching glimpses of the light of the advancing sentiment, the whole continent of Europe with Great Britain, rocking under the demand for equality without regard to sex. Our own country has given to women partial suffrage in twenty-two states; and one, Wyoming, is reaping the blessedness of the full and impartial enfranchisement of her daughters. Our own state is behind all these; but even here, we cannot escape the march onward. A crack has been opened in the door of Brown University, in response to our incessant knocking, and its worthy president proposes to make the most of this small privilege. Our antiquated prejudice against women on the boards of control of state institutions, has vanished; and women have been appointed to help establish and manage the State School for Deaf Mutes, while other women are cooperating successfully with good men in making our state home and school what it was intended to be, a place for the proper training of citizens.

And yet, with all this advancement, for which we are devoutly thankful, Rhode Island is still standing far below the high standard of justice to which her own early declarations and the civilization of the age are calling her.

Section 1st of Article 1st of our state constitution reads thus: "In the words of the Father of his country, we declare that the basis of our political systems is the right of the people to make and alter their constitutions of government; but that the constitution which at any time exists, till changed by an explicit and authentic act of the whole people, is sacredly obligatory upon all."

Section 2nd declares: "All free governments are instituted for the protection, safety and happiness of the people. All laws, therefore, should be made for the good of the whole." And, in this manner, the twenty-three sections of the 1st Article treat of the rights of "the people," often using the word "persons;" and both in a manner which any intelligent person could construe in no other way, but as including both men and women. But, when we come to Article 2nd, "Of the qualification of electors," then comes out the cloven and the cleaving foot. "Every male citizen of the United States, who has had his residence in this state for one year," etc., "shall thereafter have a right to vote," etc.

One of the chief qualifications for voting prescribed in this article is the payment of taxes. Women in Rhode Island pay taxes on near a hundred millions of dollars' worth of property; and that they are citizens, and were not forgotten, is admitted by the use of the word "male."

Section 1st of Chapter 154, which declares, "Every person authorized by law to make a will, except married women, shall have a right to appoint by will a guardian or guardians for his children during their minority." Think of that, mothers of legitimate children. Did you know that your husbands, on their death beds, if they are so disposed, may deprive you of all control over your children? I advise you to read the whole chapter concerning the powers of guardians, that you may learn how entirely the right of the mother is ignored by Rhode Island law. Then I think you will never say again, as I fear some of you have said, that you have all the rights you want. Unmarried mothers have the undisputed control of their children.

Also, I advise women to read Chapter 176, "Of descent, distribution and advancement," where it is declared that intestate estates, if there are no children of the deceased person, shall go to the father of such person, if there be a father. If there be no father, then to the mother, brothers and sisters of such person in equal portions, if any there be. If there be no mother, etc., then to the grandfather if there be one."

And so on, the male progenitor always having the advantage, if one can be found out of his grave.

Now, my dear friends, I think you will agree with me, that for us whose eyes are opened to see these great wrongs, there is no release from our labor, until women help to make the laws and establish the customs by which humanity shall be governed in its upward and onward way.

And our part in this righteous conflict, this world wide reformation, is to be faithful to our special purpose here—the enfranchisement of Rhode Island women.

• 9 •

Factory Working Conditions for Women and Girls

by Elizabeth Buffum Chace,
Written in 1881

*I*t is a fact, that a very large number of women and girls, from ten years old to forty or fifty, are employed in the cotton and woolen mills of the northern and middle states of this country, mostly in New England. It is, therefore, a subject of grave concern as to what is their actual condition, and, what are the duties of other women toward them. Many of those born in England, Ireland and Canada cannot read or write; and of those who have gone to work so early, that their schooling has been of the most rudimentary character, and is easily forgotten. They are excluded from the society of their own sex outside of the factory, by a variety of barriers—chief of which are their foreign birth or extraction, their poverty, their want of education, and the necessity that they should be always at work. Two other causes also contribute largely to this exclusion. These people are mostly Catholic in their religion, and this excludes them from Protestant companionship, as well as excludes Protestant companionship from them; and the other cause is, the growing tendency in our civilization, toward class distinctions.

Many of these operatives live in a floating life. Trifling circumstances, and the hope of improving their condition, lead them to move about, and thus they continue unthrifty and poor; and, whatever unfortunate results follow, they all bear with most hardship upon the women. On the contrary, those who remain in one place, if they cultivate habits of industry and sobriety, do constantly improve their circumstances, and become more and more assimilated to the native inhabitants. But, with rare exceptions, they have brought with them the inherited improvidence, which comes from many generations in hopeless poverty, under old world oppressions. Their grandmothers were not of the kind who never suffered a crumb that a chicken would eat, to be swept into the fire, or a piece of bread that a child could hold in his hand, to be cast into the swill-pail, or a shred of cloth that would serve for a patch, to go into the rag-bag. The vice of intemperance is a terrible curse to these people; and, though drunkenness is far less common among women than men, still, it is they who suffer most severely from its effects. The operatives are mostly women and young persons of both sexes; the men are not always able to find employment at anything they can do, and so, they often get into the habit of depending on their children for support, and, in their idleness, they indulge in drinking, which renders them a torment as well as a burden in their homes.

These homes have too often little to make them either comfortable or attractive to their inmates. The tenement system in the villages necessitates the crowding of several families in too close proximity; two and sometimes four families using the same stairs, entries and doors, making neatness and privacy impossible. In some of these tenements, the room where all the cooking, eating, washing, etc., are done, is the only sitting room, thus giving little chance for comfort, to say nothing of recreation.

Much of the poverty which we find in families who have been long employed in the factory is due to the constant employment of young girls therein, because they are thus left ignorant of all proper management of household affairs. Many of these girls cannot sew decently; they know nothing of the cutting or fitting of garments, that great source of economy in poor households. They understand little of cooking, they are wholly ignorant of hygiene, and have no idea what foods are nutritious, and, consequently, economical. They have had no time to learn, and nobody to teach them, for their mothers were ignorant before them. The need is imperative, of finding some way to teach these growing girls, who are to be the wives and mothers of future workers of both sexes, the needful art of right home-making and home-living. Where there are no sufficient accommodations for bathing indoors, the health of the women suffers more from the want the men, because men and boys have the use of the ponds and rivers. The introduction of bath-houses for the operatives, by some manufacturers, is a blessing that should be made universal, and where it has been bestowed, it is appreciated by the recipients beyond all expectation.

Ventilation in tenement houses is seldom sufficiently provided for, and, as a rule, this class of people are excessively afraid of open windows at night. The pale faces, the languid steps, noticeable in factory girls, are as much due to unhealthful conditions at home, as to overwork and confinement in the mills. And, I repeat, the important necessity is, the securing of time and opportunity to the girls for learning the arts of healthful, frugal housekeeping.

A girl who goes into the mill at twelve years of age, and I am sorry to have to say they often do when younger, and works there till she marries; and, as is frequently the case, continues to work there until she has children, and often afterward leaves some old woman to care for the little ones while she goes to the factory for ten or eleven hours a day, cannot, in the nature of things, become a wise and prudent housewife.

The question of the employment of young children in the factories is of so difficult solution that one meets with great discouragement at the outset in any undertaking to prevent it. The first obstacle which strikes the humane student of factory life, after the conviction that young children should not work there, is the apparent necessity that they must do so or be worse off than they are. They often belong to large families, in which there are several children younger than themselves; the mother has her hands full, with the nursing and the housework; the wages of the father will not support the family, even if he dispenses with the expense of tobacco and rum. Thus, it often happens, that the labor of such children is so important an item in the maintenance of the household, that one is unable to see how it can be dispensed with. I have, myself, with the best intention of preventing young children from being permitted to work, lacked the courage to interfere, when it seemed quite certain that such interference must ensure their actual suffering and that of the other members of their families, or compel them to depend on charity. In all the New England states, laws have been enacted and amended, from time to time, to limit and regulate the employment of children in manufacturing establishments. In Massachusetts the law forbids such employment of any child under ten years of age, with heavy penalty upon any parent or guardian who violates it. Also, the employment of any child under fourteen, unless such child shall attend school twenty weeks in each year. Truant officers are appointed in every manufacturing town, to see that the law is enforced; and I believe it is more fully attended to in Massachusetts than in any other state. Still, violations are frequently reported at Fall River, while at Lowell, it is claimed that the law is strictly obeyed, as far as is possible; and that the superintendents of the corporations and the school teachers cooperate with the authorities in the matter. And yet, the superintendent of the Merrimack Mills says, that he has no doubt they have many children at work below the age of ten years, because mother and child will swear to the requisite age, and so, with all their vigilance, the authorities are foiled. In Maine, the law is scarcely less stringent, and yet, ex-Governor Dingley declares, that "it is not enforced, except in special cases—as when the School Committee" (who are the only persons appointed to attend to it) "make a special request to the agents"—and from the tone of the answer of Governor Dingley, I judge this is but seldom. Connecticut, New Hampshire and Rhode Island statutes differ only slightly from the preceding; but I fear they are not very rigidly enforced or obeyed, except as the manufacturers choose to observe them. I am sure this is the case in Rhode Island; although there is a movement here in the direction of more stringent measures, which is not yet put into law. For reasons heretofore stated, there is not, as a general rule, in most manufacturing places, any hearty cooperation with the authorities, on the part of the parents, in the fact that they do not know the physical deterioration which must result to their offspring from too early continual labor; and they do not appreciate the value of the education which their children are thus deprived of. Also, these parents are, in many cases, miserably poor. The father is often intemperate, and the mother, dragged about from one factory village to another, too frequently adding more children to the burden she already carries, learns to calculate upon their earnings, as fast as they get old enough to use their hands. For all this, the employer is not wholly responsible. Partly in charity and kindness, partly because such labor is cheaper, partly because some work in factories can best be done by children, and partly from indifference and inattention, it is seldom that the employers themselves take any decisive measures to secure obedience to these laws. The laws themselves, although intended for protection of the children, do not sufficiently protect them, because continuous labor of this character, from ten to eleven hours a day, is too much for any children under sixteen years of age, even for nine months in the year; and many of those so employed are not over ten or twelve. The moral, economical, physical and mental effect is injurious, and, therefore, although temporarily beneficial in the support of the families, it is, in the end, unprofitable to all concerned. Also, in many cases, the effect upon parents of depending upon their young children for support is bad. Drunken, idle fathers, drunken, negligent mothers are to be found in this class or our population, who learn to depend easily on the labor of young boys and girls for bread, as well as for rum and tobacco.

I shall, of course, in this paper especially consider only the effect of this juvenile labor upon girls, leaving the question of its results upon the growing manhood to be discussed on other occasions.

Most of the work performed by girls in factories requires almost constant standing; and of course some of it is more difficult than others. A superintendent of many years' experience told me that the work on one kind of machine, performed entirely by girls of thirteen and fourteen years, is, with one exception, considering the nature of the labor and the strength of the laborers, the most difficult and the most straining of any work done in a cotton mill. And the exception is some work performed by men. When I asked him why boys were not set to do this work, he replied, that it required a nimbleness and dexterity of the fingers, of which only young girls are capable. And yet it is absolutely legal to employ these girls in this standing, straining work, which requires this constant and swift motion of the hands either ten or eleven hours a day, for nine months in the year. Fortunately, in each cotton mill, there are but few required on this particular machine, and most of the girls can gain time to take some rest during every day. But many girls, at that critical age, are employed in other tasks, which, though less arduous, do keep them on their feet the greater part of the time; although at this day, seats are pretty generally provided for them to use in spare moments.

Many physicians, of late years, have sounded the alarm concerning overstudy, schoolhouses built in such a manner as to necessitate the climbing of many stairs by young girls, and other causes of ill-health among them. These evils affect the more carefully guarded classes of children, belonging to families, where, in other respects, hygiene is more or less considered, and youth receives some protection, in the effort to establish a vigorous womanhood. The girls for whom I speak come from another class, who, in other respects, have little chance for health, who sleep in ill-ventilated rooms, who eat unwholesome food, who are often poorly clad, and upon whose dawning womanhood is laid this fearful strain.

It seems to me a vain excuse to say that such is an unavoidable result of financial laws, which require that the working classes shall be worked to the utmost extent of their strength. If the controlling classes, in their struggle to retain and increase their wealth, are justified in availing themselves of all the power given them by the possession of capital, of all the forces created by what are called the laws of trade, to the detriment of their weaker fellow-creatures, I see no reason why they would not also be justified in using physical force to attain the same end, thus converting their employees into chattel slaves. Neither can the urgency of competition justify us in "laying heavy burdens grievous to be borne" upon shoulders too weak to carry them healthfully.

If manufacturers would make their superintendents and overseers understand that they desire the welfare of the help more than the greatest amount of labor, much good would result. A superintendent said to me, "A man in my position is between two duties; he doesn't want to crowd work on an operative that he knows will nearly kill him, and yet he feels under an obligation to the manufacturer to get all the work done possible."

Studying this question of juvenile labor in all its aspects, the only just solution which seems to me possible is the general establishment by law of half-time schools, to be maintained at the public expense, and made a branch of the public school system. Thus, there could be two sets of children to attend the same machinery, one in the forenoon and the other in the afternoon, alternating the attendance at school in the same way; and this, of course, should be made compulsory. By this means the children would be receiving a double education—one in the very important art of being useful and of earning a living; the other in the knowledge and wisdom of the school, so necessary to the proper development of character and the making of worthy citizens. This system, as adopted and tried in England, is pronounced entirely satisfactory. These families of factory workers must have the help of their children, and our present system, even where the restraining laws are best enforced, as they are, I believe, in Massachusetts, do not overcome all the objectionable features in the employment of these children. And where they are not thoroughly enforced, as I know to be the case in Rhode Island, we are allowing to grow up, a large class of dwarfed and ignorant people, which gives anything but promise for the future welfare of our country, to say nothing of the cruel injustice of such a system to the people themselves. It is asserted, as the result of experience with half-time schools, that children so taught learn more rapidly and have more liking for the school than do those who are confined there the whole of the school day; and also that they have more interest and more activity and faithfulness in their work when their working time is so shortened that is does not weary them. All which seems rational. Evening schools for children employed throughout the day, though better than none, must always be a partial failure, because preceded by a full day's work, which unfits the mind for much mental activity.

An important subject to be considered in this connection is the virtue of factory girls. In this, perhaps, more than in any other class of society, it is impossible to be sure of preserving the purity of the maidens, while no effort is made to inculcate an equal morality into the minds of the boys who grow up beside them. These young men have no lower class of women upon whom to prey, and, if their passions are uncontrolled by moral principle, their influence upon the girls with whom they are in daily and hourly association is of the most dangerous character.

Both tenement and factory life tend to break reserve between the sexes, and, when the girls are only slightly guarded and imperfectly taught, and the boys are neither guarded nor taught at all, the result is natural. There is, of course, a large class of factory families in which virtue is taught and respected, and where the daughters are as carefully trained and watched over, as the circumstances will permit; but, in the more ignorant and wretched families, where the parents are frequently intemperate, and the children rush gladly, when the day's work is done, into the streets, away from their crowded and unclean homes, it is not strange that the sensual instincts assume control. The discomforts of many of the homes, sometimes extending to actual cruelty by drunken parents toward their children, not infrequently sends the daughters out to become an easy prey to any solicitations which wear the garb of tenderness and gentleness, and which come from the sex, who, in the eyes of the world, suffer little disrepute thereby.

Another source of temptation is the fact, that girls who live at home, whether they are of age or not, rarely have the control of their own wages. Instead of paying their board to their parents, and reserving the rest to use at their own discretion, it is the almost invariable custom for the mother to take all that the daughters earn, and then provide them such clothing as she thinks she can spare from the family necessities. I have known girls long past their majority, who had worked in the mill from their childhood, but had never had a cent they could call their own. Notwithstanding all these untoward circumstances, I believe it is rare that a factory girl becomes an actual prostitute; and though less mercenary lapses from virtue, often followed by wretched marriages, do occur, there is still much to be said in praise and commendation of the lives of many of these girls. Better homes, wiser teaching, for the youth of both sexes, would do much to prevent the currents of their young lives from setting in wrong directions, into which too many of them naturally enter, when it is almost the only relief from toil, and the sole change from dreary conditions of existence. With experienced, conscientious teachers, I should hope much from the half-time schools, for the moral training of this, to me, deeply interesting class of people.

In depicting the condition of women and girls, both in the factory and the home, I wish it to be understood, that much of what I say is the result of my own personal observation. Also, I do not mean to give the impression, that the employment of large numbers of women and men, in establishments for the manufacture of useful fabrics, is, in itself, an evil. Neither do I mean that the wrong conditions of which I speak are equally in force in all manufactories, although I do believe they exist in all to some extent. There are many cases, where constant attempts are made by manufacturers to correct abuses, and to improve the condition and elevate the character of the operatives.

In factory homes a frequent visitor will often meet with incidents and circumstances that reveal conditions from which there is much to hope. I have, myself, witnessed instances of rare cleanliness and tastefulness, under very unfavorable circumstances, and evidences of unselfishness and kindness, such as is seldom to be found elsewhere. Living as these people generally do, in tenements so connected, that the different families are constantly coming in contact in all their domestic affairs, the numerous children being much together, from all parts of the house, there have been times when I have bowed my head in humiliation and reverence, before the forbearance, the self-denial and the patient endurance of some of these women. Unless incited by intoxicating drinks, a quarrel between different families is a rare occurrence.

There is another class of factory women, to whom I have hitherto made no allusion, but to whom I should be very unjust, if I failed to include them in the considerations of this paper; and that is, the wives and daughters of the manufacturers. In this day of larger establishments, of greater wealth and higher opportunities, they are not required to take part in the running of the machinery; but, in the light of a searching analysis of duty, they cannot be excused from a grave responsibility in the process of dealing with the concerns of those from the results of whose labor, they largely derive the means of their own comfort and enjoyment.

The ascent from ignorance, poverty, coarseness and hardship, to culture, wealth, refinement and ease, is by slow steps of progress, and those at the highest point are fortunate in having had the way opened for them by others who have preceded them. And surely it is their duty to hold out to those behind them a helping hand, in order to lift them as far as possible to a level with themselves. I know plenty of people, who are now in the enjoyment of all the advantages which wealth bestows, whose grandparents were, within my own memory, among the handworkers of the day; some of them as uneducated and as poor as are many of those now employed by their grandchildren. There is much these more fortunate women can do to improve the conditions in the lives of their humbler sisters; and, as the recipients of the fruits of their labor, there is no excuse for them if they pass them by on the other side. These factory women of the higher class should make themselves personally acquainted with the actual condition of the feminine workers in the mills. It is their duty to see that too heavy work is not required of them; that they have seats on which to rest in spare moments; and, above all, that the superintendents and overseers are men who, while they are qualified to manage the work well, are also morally fit to preside over women and girls. If this better class of factory women would combine in any one state, to secure the establishment of half-time schools, I believe they would be successful. When this is accomplished, the time thus gained will afford opportunity to institute cooking schools, sewing schools and kitchen gardens, where the young girls can be trained for housekeeping. These upper class factory women should visit the homes and take a personal interest in their concerns. Many suggestions they might make there would be invaluable to these households. Their very presence and their kindly words would give comfort and hope to the hearts of the women they would meet there. The little children in the families of the factory workers should be the especial care of these ladies, who should establish nurseries and kindergartens, to save from neglect in the homes and contamination in the streets, these future men and women, whose lives are often turned in wrong directions before they are old enough to be admitted to the schools. To my sisters of this fortunate class of factory women, I would urge an appeal, if I could, that should banish sleep from their eyes and slumber from their eyelids, until they were so awakened to a sense of their duties, as to lead them to go forth to the investigation of the condition of every family, and of every woman, and of every girl, whose labor in the mill, while it produces the means of their own support, helps also to furnish the supply of purple and fine linen which these ladies wear. What better supplement to the education of a young lady could there be, than the round of visiting by her mother's side, which this service would require? To what better purpose could she devote a share of her leisure time, than to devising and carrying out methods for the amusement, instruction and benefit, in a variety of ways, of the young girls, whose lives could be sweetened and enriched by her sisterly ministrations; while, from some of them, she could learn lessons of self-sacrifice and faithfulness in the performance of duty, such as her life has hitherto given her no opportunity to conceive?

I would not exclude from such beneficence other women living in factory neighborhoods, who are not directly interested in the financial interests of the mills, but who, with their children, cannot escape the effect of the moral, intellectual and physical atmosphere around them. I maintain that, wherever we live, it is our duty to interest ourselves in the welfare of the people among whom our lives are cast, especially if in the race of progress, they are behind us; and this for our own sake as well as theirs. We cannot flee from our responsibilities of this character, and woe be unto us if we ignore them. The plea that the people around us are not in our employ, and therefore we have no duties toward them, will not save us from the consequences to ourselves of our neglect of them. The unfortunate Jew who fell among thieves was not only an alien but he was an enemy of the good Samaritan who ministered to his necessities.

When I read, some weeks ago, in the report of the day's proceedings in the General Assembly, that "an amused smile passed over the countenances of the senators as Senator Baker presented the Memorial of the Rhode Island Woman Suffrage Association," I wondered if the consciences of the legislators of Rhode Island could ever be awakened to a sense of their continual violation of the principles of our government as well as of the Golden Rule.

• Appendix •
Buffum Family Genealogy

Researched and Designed
by Lucille Salitan

FIRST GENERATION

Born–1741   **William Buffum** m. Lydia Arnold (1)
(grandfather of the sisters)

	Patience
	Hannah
	Lucy
	Thomas
1782	Arnold (2)
	Wait
	Martha
	Lydia
	William

SECOND GENERATION

Arnold Buffum m. Rebecca Gould (2)
(father of the sisters)

1804	Sarah (3)
1806	Elizabeth (4)
1809	Lucy (5)
1811	Rebecca (6)
	John
1815	Lydia (7)
	Mary
	William Penn
1821	William (8)
1823	Edward (9)

Each person who was followed until marriage has a number following his/her name which is repeated after the marriage listing. Children are listed beneath the marriage listing of their parents. Those persons without numbers either died before marriage or could not be traced.

THIRD GENERATION
(sisters and brothers)

Sarah Buffum m. Nathaniel Borden (3)

Elizabeth Buffum m. Samuel Chace (4)
> Samuel
> Oliver
> John
> Edward
> Arnold (10)
> Mary (11)
> Lillie (12)

Lucy Buffum m. Rev. Nehemiah Lovell (5)
> Caroline
> Laura
> Edward
> William (13)
> Shubael
> Lucy

Rebecca Buffum m. Marcus Spring (6)

Lydia Buffum m. Clement Read (7)
> Sara (14)

William Buffum m. Marian Simmons (8)

Edward Buffum m. Eliza Wilkinson (9)

FOURTH GENERATION
(children of the sisters)

Arnold Chace m. Elizabeth Greene (10)
> Arnold, Jr. (15)
> 1875   Malcolm (16)
> Margaret Lillie
> Edward (17)

Mary Chace m. Horace Cheney (11)
> m. James Tolman
> Elizabeth
> Richard
> Edward

Lillie Chace m. Arthur Wyman (12)

William Lovell (13) m. Sara Read (14)
    1890   Malcolm (18)
               Bertha
               Edith
               Mildred

FIFTH GENERATION
(grandchildren of the sisters)

Arnold Chace, Jr. m. Alice Perkins (15)
                  m. Anne Palm
        Jonathan (19)

Malcolm Chace m. Elizabeth Edwards (16)
                 m. Kathleen Dunster
    1904   Malcolm, Jr. (20)
    1906   Eliot
    1909   Jane
    1911   Elizabeth
    1914   Arnold (21)

Edward Chace m. Christine ~~McLeod~~ MAC (17)
    1910   Christine
    1913   Eliza~~beth~~
    1914   Jessie

Malcolm Lovell m. Emily Monihan (18)
                 m. Juanita West
        Malcolm, Jr. (22)
    1937   Arnold (23)

SIXTH GENERATION
(great-grandchildren of the sisters)

Jonathan Chace m. Ruth Halstead (19)

Malcolm Chace, Jr. m. Beatrice Olnslager (20)
    1934   Malcolm, III (24)
               Jane
    1932   Eliot

Arnold Chace m. Evelyn (21)
    1947   Arnold, Jr. (29)

Malcolm Lovell, Jr. m. Martha Sheldon (22)
                           m. Beatrice Sweeney
                           m. Celia Coghlan

1950	Lucie (25)
1953	Sara (26)
1956	Annette (27)
1959	Caroline (28)

Arnold Lovell m. Amanda Norris (23)

1964	Jonathan
1969	William

SEVENTH GENERATION
(great-great-grandchildren of the sisters)

Malcolm Chace, III m. Barbara Burding (24)
                           m. Elizabeth Zophi

1967	Malcolm, IV
1966	Elizabeth
1968	Barbara

Arnold Chace, Jr. m. Jonnie (29)

1983 <	Arnold, III
	Sara
1986	Nathaniel
1989	Elizabeth

Lucie Lovell m. Steven Tillson (25)

1982	Alexander
1985	Rebecka
1988	Katherine

Sara Lovell m. Elliott Birckhead (26)

1986	Elliott
1988	Emily

Annette Lovell m. Christopher Nathan (27)

1992	Nicholas
1993	Adam

Caroline Lovell m. Mark Malmberg (28)

1987	Henry
1990	Arlo